SMART FINANCE

SMART FINANCE

LEVERAGING AI FOR ENHANCED FINANCIAL PLANNING AND ANALYSIS

CHRISTIAN MARTINEZ

WILEY

This edition first published 2026

© 2026 John Wiley & Sons, Ltd

All rights reserved, including rights for text and data mining and training of artificial intelligence technologies or similar technologies. No part of this publication may be reproduced, stored in a retrieval system, or transmitted, in any form or by any means, electronic, mechanical, photocopying, recording or otherwise, except as permitted by law. Advice on how to obtain permission to reuse material from this title is available at http://www.wiley.com/go/permissions.

The right of Christian Martinez to be identified as the author of this work has been asserted in accordance with law.

Registered Offices
John Wiley & Sons, Inc., 111 River Street, Hoboken, NJ 07030, USA

John Wiley & Sons Ltd, New Era House, 8 Oldlands Way, Bognor Regis, West Sussex, PO22 9NQ, UK

For details of our global editorial offices, customer services, and more information about Wiley products visit us at www.wiley.com.

The manufacturer's authorized representative according to the EU General Product Safety Regulation is Wiley-VCH GmbH, Boschstr. 12, 69469 Weinheim, Germany, e-mail: Product_Safety@wiley.com.

Wiley also publishes its books in a variety of electronic formats and by print-on-demand. Some content that appears in standard print versions of this book may not be available in other formats.

Trademarks: Wiley and the Wiley logo are trademarks or registered trademarks of John Wiley & Sons, Inc. and/or its affiliates in the United States and other countries and may not be used without written permission. All other trademarks are the property of their respective owners. John Wiley & Sons, Inc. is not associated with any product or vendor mentioned in this book.

Limit of Liability/Disclaimer of Warranty
While the publisher and the authors have used their best efforts in preparing this work, including a review of the content of the work, neither the publisher nor the authors make any representations or warranties with respect to the accuracy or completeness of the contents of this work and specifically disclaim all warranties, including without limitation any implied warranties of merchantability or fitness for a particular purpose. Certain AI systems have been used in the creation of this work. No warranty may be created or extended by sales representatives, written sales materials or promotional statements for this work. The fact that an organization, website, or product is referred to in this work as a citation and/or potential source of further information does not mean that the publisher and authors endorse the information or services the organization, website, or product may provide or recommendations it may make. This work is sold with the understanding that the publisher is not engaged in rendering professional services. The advice and strategies contained herein may not be suitable for your situation. You should consult with a specialist where appropriate. Further, readers should be aware that websites listed in this work may have changed or disappeared between when this work was written and when it is read. Neither the publisher nor authors shall be liable for any loss of profit or any other commercial damages, including but not limited to special, incidental, consequential, or other damages.

Library of Congress Cataloging-in-Publication Data is Available:

ISBN 9781394369164 (Cloth)
ISBN 9781394369171 (ePub)
ISBN 9781394369188 (ePDF)

Cover Design: Wiley
Author Photo: Courtesy of Christian Martinez

Set in 12.5/15 pts and Bembo Std by Straive, Chennai, India.

Printed and bound by CPI Group (UK) Ltd, Croydon, CR0 4YY

To my mum, Teresa, thank you for all your support and love throughout my life.

To my partner, Holly, you are my best friend and life companion.

Portions of this text were drafted with assistance from ChatGPT4o by OpenAI. This AI tool helped organize my ideas, suggest alternative phrasing for complex concepts, and improve clarity and conciseness throughout the writing process. All AI-generated content was carefully reviewed, edited, and approved.

Contents

Chapter 1	The AI Revolution in Finance	1
Chapter 2	Prompt Engineering for Finance Professionals	21
Chapter 3	Teaching AI to Code—Without Being a Programmer	57
Chapter 4	Descriptive Analytics—Let AI Do the Reporting	79
Chapter 5	From "What Happened?" to "Why Did It Happen?"	103
Chapter 6	Predictive Analytics	125
Chapter 7	Prescriptive Analytics—From Insight to Action	151
Chapter 8	Automation in FP&A—Doing More with Less	177

Chapter 9	Building Your AI Finance Stack	207
Chapter 10	Becoming an AI-Enabled Finance Leader	231
About the Author		253
Index		255

Chapter 1

The AI Revolution in Finance

The Shift AI Is Creating in Finance

The role of finance is changing, and so is the way finance professionals work. Artificial intelligence (AI) is no longer a futuristic tool; it is a mainstream one that is reshaping how analysis, planning, communication, and decision-making happen in organizations of every size.

For those of us in financial planning and analysis (FP&A), this change is especially acute. FP&A has always been about finding patterns in data, making sense of complexity, and helping organizations navigate uncertainty.

But the speed at which those expectations are rising—faster insights, tighter deadlines, more strategic recommendations—has outpaced traditional tools and methods.

This is where AI enters the scene. Whether it's summarizing monthly performance, generating commentary, cleaning messy data, forecasting future cash flows, or even writing Python scripts to automate repetitive tasks, AI is offering finance professionals an entirely new set of capabilities.

And the change is not coming—it's already here.

To understand this shift, think about the introduction of Microsoft Excel. When Excel was first released, it wasn't immediately adopted by everyone in finance. Some people experimented with it. Some resisted it. Many assumed it would be a passing trend or something for the IT team to worry about.

But those who learned how to use Excel early on unlocked new levels of speed, accuracy, and insight. They became the go-to problem-solvers. They were promoted faster, valued more, and often given more strategic work to do.

Over time, Excel became table stakes. Today, it is unthinkable to work in FP&A without knowing how to use Excel competently.

AI is at that same inflection point today.

Right now, finance teams are seeing the early adopters use AI to speed up variance commentary, automate reports, generate visualizations, and write custom code for reconciliation checks.

It might feel unfamiliar or even threatening—but so did spreadsheets once. The question is not whether AI will become embedded in our daily work. It's how quickly you're willing to adapt to it—and how soon you'll start using it to your advantage.

The future of finance is not about replacement. It's about reinforcement.

AI will not take your job. But a finance professional who knows how to use AI probably will outpace you.

This might sound stark, but it's already happening. I've seen junior analysts producing executive-level dashboards in a fraction of the time it used to take. I've seen FP&A managers reduce their month-end cycle from 10 days to 4. I've worked with chief financial officers (CFOs) who now draft board commentary with the help of generative AI in half the time, using language models that tailor output to their preferred tone.

These aren't experiments—they are real changes, already underway.

That's why this book exists. It's not about convincing you that AI is useful. It's about giving you the tools and thinking patterns to make it part of your work. It's about showing you that you don't need to be a programmer or a data scientist to use AI.

You just need to learn how to ask better questions, structure your prompts clearly, and use the tools that are now at your fingertips.

If Excel was the 1990s productivity leap for finance, AI is the 2020s leap. But the window for early adoption is short. In a few years, working without AI in FP&A will be as limiting as working without Excel is today.

This is your opportunity to move early. To lead the next generation of finance professionals. To evolve—not away from what makes finance valuable but toward a version of finance that's faster, sharper, and better equipped for today's business environment.

Welcome to the shift. Welcome to AI-powered finance.

My Journey into AI-Powered Finance

My own journey into AI didn't begin with a breakthrough moment—it began with a question: How can finance be done better?

In 2016, I began a master's program in finance at Monash Business School in Melbourne. It wasn't just finance I was interested in—it was the intersection of finance and data. I chose the data science specialization because I wanted to understand not just how to interpret financial results but how to use data, models, and systems to anticipate and influence them. That dual focus shaped the path I've taken ever since.

Since completing that degree, I've spent over eight years in finance roles across two continents: Australia and Europe, specifically the Netherlands. I've worked as a site controller for a large-scale factory operation managing multimillion-dollar budgets, as an FP&A analyst building scenario models under pressure, and most recently as a senior manager leading global finance transformation. My teams support over 20 global markets. My scope includes finance analytics, automation, forecasting, controllership, and reporting. I present directly to CFOs and controllers and build the tools that their decisions rely on.

But it wasn't until the end of 2022 that everything accelerated.

When OpenAI released ChatGPT 3.5 in November 2022, I immediately recognized the shift. Suddenly, many of the capabilities I had been using behind the scenes—forecasting algorithms, text generation, code automation—were available through a simple chat interface. No Python setup. No API authentication. Just a prompt. It was as if the command line had been replaced with a conversation.

From that point on, I became obsessed—with possibility, with capability, and with sharing what I was learning. I started testing tools daily. I built workflows, wrote code with AI, debugged its outputs, and experimented with new models. I spoke with finance professionals from around the world about their needs. I learned what was working, what was overhyped, and where the real impact was happening.

In 2023, I launched a global training initiative with Nicolas Boucher, a fellow thought leader in this space. Together, we've delivered 14 cohorts of our Advanced AI for Finance program, training professionals from leading companies in Europe, the Americas, Asia, and Australia. These sessions were more than instructional—they were collaborative, intense, and grounded in reality. We tested use cases, shared breakthroughs, and iterated on techniques week by week. That program continues to grow, and it has become a proving ground for how AI can be practically applied inside finance teams of all shapes and sizes.

I've also trained over 15,000 professionals through my three LinkedIn Learning courses, focused on Python, machine learning (ML), and automation in finance. The feedback from these learners has been invaluable—and eye-opening. People want to learn this. They want to adapt. But they need someone who understands both the technical side and the day-to-day reality of working in finance.

I've spoken at major conferences across the world—from Australia to the Netherlands. My talks have covered the future of finance, the real-world application of AI in corporate settings, and what it means to lead in a time of massive transformation. These moments, whether onstage or in small workshops with CFOs, have only deepened my commitment to this work.

Because this isn't theoretical for me. I don't write about AI in finance from the outside. I live it. I build the tools. I deploy the models. I present the insights. I help teams adopt them. And I teach others how to do the same.

This book is the result of those years of experimentation, teaching, testing, and real-world implementation. It's not about hype. It's about helping finance professionals understand what's possible—and then giving them the tools, language, and techniques to act on it.

AI is no longer reserved for engineers and PhDs. It belongs to finance professionals, too. You just need the right guide.

What This Book Covers and Who It's For

This book is written for one very specific audience: finance professionals who are ready to embrace the next wave of tools, but don't want to waste time on theory, hype, or abstract models that don't apply to their work.

It's for the CFO who wants to make the finance function more agile, accurate, and forward-looking. For the FP&A manager who's juggling three overlapping forecasts, multiple stakeholder requests, and a sea of disconnected spreadsheets. For the financial analyst who's already thinking, "There has to be a faster way." And for the controller who wants to automate routine processes while keeping governance and accuracy intact.

This is not just a book about the future of finance—it's about the present and how to make the future available for you and your organization.

These tools are available now. They are usable now. And when applied intentionally, they deliver value immediately.

But AI can be overwhelming. There are too many tools. Too many claims. Too many promises of 10× productivity without any clarity on where to start or how to make it real in the flow of day-to-day finance work.

That's where this book comes in.

What you'll find here is a clear, focused road map for using AI in FP&A—from operational tasks to strategic decision-making.

Every chapter is built on real-world workflows and use cases I've seen in practice, taught in classrooms, or implemented inside companies.

You'll learn how to do the following:

- Use generative AI tools like ChatGPT, Gemini, and Microsoft Copilot to write commentary, summarize performance, and build management decks.
- Work through prompt engineering techniques tailored to finance so you know how to get the outputs you need faster and more reliably.
- Get AI to write Python code for you: scripts to clean data, merge datasets, automate reports, run forecasts, or analyze trends.
- Apply AI to the four levels of analytics: descriptive, diagnostic, predictive, and prescriptive, all within the context of finance work.
- Automate repetitive workflows using both code-based and no-code tools like Power Query, n8n, and Make.
- Build lightweight AI agents that can act on triggers, generate reports, or respond to financial questions dynamically.
- Train your team and shape your finance function to be AI-enabled so you're not just doing it yourself, but bringing others along.

You don't need to have a data science background.
You don't need to know how to write Python from scratch.

You don't need to be technical.

You just need to know how to ask—and that's where AI comes alive.

The goal of this book is to demystify AI, but also to operationalize it. If all you do is read and understand what's possible, that's a start. But if you apply what you learn—if you build your first automation, run your first AI-generated forecast, or reduce a repetitive monthly task to a single AI prompt—then you're already ahead of the curve.

Because AI isn't just another tool. It's a new way of working. And it's already becoming a competitive advantage in finance.

Understanding AI, ML, Generative AI, and LLMs

Before diving into applications, it's essential to build a shared understanding of the core technologies shaping this shift. You don't need to become an AI engineer or a data scientist but I believe you do need to know what these systems are, what they do, and why they're changing how finance works.

Let's break it down—starting from the top.

AI

AI is a broad term. At its core, AI refers to machines or systems that can perform tasks normally requiring human intelligence. This includes activities like reasoning, learning, problem-solving, language understanding, and pattern recognition.

In practical terms, AI powers the tools that help us write commentary, forecast trends, automate dashboards, or flag anomalies in financial data. The algorithms themselves are invisible, but their effects are not. If you've ever used a tool that auto-completes your sentence, suggests a formula, or categorizes data based on behavior, you've interacted with AI.

AI isn't one technology. It's a field of study and development made up of many techniques—and one of the most powerful branches is ML.

ML

ML is a subset of AI. It enables systems to learn from data without being explicitly programmed. Instead of writing a rule for every possible situation (like "if sales increase by x, then do y"), ML enables computers to learn patterns directly from data. You give the system historical inputs and outcomes—like revenue, marketing spend, and seasonality—and it figures out the relationships on its own.

Then, it can make predictions or classifications on new data.

For finance, this is incredibly powerful. You can use ML to do the following:

- Forecast revenue, costs, or cash flow.
- Detect anomalies in transactions.
- Cluster similar accounts or suppliers.
- Predict default risks or budget overruns.
- Classify commentary by theme or sentiment.

ML works best when there is a large volume of structured data, historical trends, and a clear outcome to predict.

Types of ML

There are three major categories of ML you'll encounter:

1. **Supervised learning:** This is the most common form. You give the algorithm labeled data—inputs and known outputs—and it learns the mapping between them.

    Example: You feed in five years of historical sales and marketing data, and the model learns how to predict next month's sales.

2. **Unsupervised learning:** Here, you give the model data without labeled outcomes. The goal is to discover hidden patterns, groupings, or structures.

Example: You give the model a dataset of spending across departments. It might identify clusters of departments with similar cost behavior or detect outliers that don't match the pattern.
3. **Reinforcement learning:** Less common in finance but growing in use. The model learns by interacting with an environment and receiving feedback in the form of rewards or penalties.

Example: You create a budget optimizer that continuously adjusts spend across cost centers to maximize return on investment, learning over time, based on performance outcomes.

Each method has its strengths. For finance teams, supervised learning tends to be the most accessible and practical starting point.

Generative AI

If ML helps you make predictions, generative AI helps you create things—text, code, visuals, and even structured data.

It's called *generative* because it generates content. And it does so by learning from large amounts of data, then producing something new that follows similar patterns.

The most well-known generative AI tools today are language models—AI systems trained to understand and produce human language.

Tools like ChatGPT, Gemini, Copilot, Claude, and others are built on this kind of AI.

For finance, this changes the game:

- You can ask generative AI to write a first draft of your monthly commentary.
- You can paste in messy data and ask it to clean, sort, or summarize it.
- You can generate Python or SQL code just by describing the task.

- You can simulate a Q&A session with your Profit and Loss division.
- You can even build scenario narratives based on business inputs.

In finance, one of the main reasons generative AI is so revolutionary is because it shifts the barrier of entry. You don't need to know code, statistical models, or scripting.

You just need to know how to ask questions clearly. And when you do, the output you get back is coherent, relevant, and—often—actionable.

The technology behind this leap is the large language model, or LLM.

LLMs

An LLM is a type of AI trained on massive amounts of text—from books, websites, financial reports, scientific papers, and more. It's designed to understand the structure and meaning of language and generate human-like responses.

Think of an LLM like an ultra-advanced autocomplete engine. But instead of just predicting your next word, it can generate entire paragraphs, explain concepts, write code, answer complex questions, and analyze data.

Here are some of the most well-known LLMs:

- GPT-4o and o3 (used in ChatGPT)
- Gemini 2.5 (developed by Google)
- LLaMA (from Meta, more open-source focused)

The key thing to understand is this: LLMs are the engine behind the conversational AI you interact with. When you type into ChatGPT or Copilot, you're interacting with a model that has digested billions of words and learned patterns of how humans speak, write, explain, and reason.

These models are not databases. They don't look up answers.

They generate responses by predicting what comes next based on your prompt and the patterns they've learned. That's why how you prompt—how you phrase your request—matters so much.

The Transformers Architecture

Behind LLMs is a technical breakthrough called the *transformer architecture*—developed by Google in 2017.

Without going too deep, this innovation allowed models to do the following:

- Understand context over long passages of text.
- Process information in parallel (which made training feasible).
- Learn relationships between words, phrases, and concepts.

Transformers revolutionized natural language processing because they enabled models to not just read text but to *understand the meaning behind it*. This is what enables a tool like ChatGPT to summarize a balance sheet, analyze commentary tone, or simulate a conversation with a fictional CFO.

Why does this matter to finance?

Because now we have systems that can do the following:

- Read and understand Excel tables.
- Follow the structure of a financial report.
- Replicate your writing tone.
- Generate code that manipulates data in a spreadsheet, SQL database, or Python notebook.
- Interpret and rewrite narratives with clarity and professionalism.

Why These Technologies Matter in Finance

Let's bring this back to day-to-day finance work. We deal with numbers, yes—but more often, we deal with the *narratives about numbers*. We communicate. We report. We explain. We analyze what changed, why it changed, and what might happen next.

AI technologies like generative models and ML accelerate and elevate this work.

- **Text generation:** Drafting performance commentary, board notes, risk assessments
- **Code generation:** Automating Excel, Power BI, or Python workflows
- **Data transformation:** Cleaning, reshaping, and interpreting messy data
- **Scenario building:** Creating narratives for what-if assumptions
- **Workflow automation:** Triggering tasks based on financial events or exceptions

You don't need to write algorithms. But you do need to know what these systems can do—and how to communicate with them.

Why Python Is the Core Skill—and How AI Makes It Accessible

If there's one technical skill that has completely changed how I work in finance, it's Python.

I first learned Python during my master's program in finance and data science in Australia. At the time, it felt like a tool built for engineers or quants.

Most of the finance professionals I met back in the day had never heard of it, let alone tried to use it. But once I saw what it could do—how it could automate repetitive tasks, build powerful forecasting models, and make dashboards dynamic—I knew I couldn't go back.

I started teaching it to colleagues, showing them how they could cut reporting time in half or run scenarios without spending hours on spreadsheets.

It wasn't easy at first. Python had a learning curve. I had to understand syntax, logic structures, functions, and environments. I made mistakes. But it was worth it. It gave me leverage. I went from being someone who built models to someone who built systems—tools that others used, reused, and built on.

For years, I encouraged finance professionals to learn at least a little bit of Python. And while many were interested, the barrier to entry always felt a bit too steep. Too technical. Too much setup. Too far from the tools they used every day.

But then everything changed with ChatGPT.

With the release of LLMs, you no longer need to learn the entire Python language to use its power.

You can simply describe what you want to do in plain language—and the AI writes the code for you. If you're clear in your prompt, if you know what you're trying to achieve, and if you're willing to iterate, you can use Python today.

No technical background required.

AI has become the bridge between finance professionals and code.

You still need to understand the basics: what input data you're using, what you want to calculate, where to paste the code. But the syntax, structure, and logic—AI takes care of that. And when it gets it wrong, you can just ask it to fix the error, explain the issue, or rewrite the code in a different way.

That's why this book includes Python-based solutions—but always through the lens of AI prompting. You won't be asked to write code from scratch. You'll learn how to ask the right questions, test the responses, and slot them into your workflows.

And today, using Python is easier than ever.

Throughout this book, I'll recommend using Google Colab. It's free, cloud-based, and requires no downloads or installations. You can open a notebook in your browser, paste in AI-generated code, run it, and see results instantly.

If you're familiar with Microsoft products and prefer a desktop setup, Visual Studio Code is a strong alternative—flexible and widely supported.

Even more exciting for finance professionals is the new integration of Python directly inside Excel.

Microsoft has launched Python in Excel as a native feature. Now, you can type =PY(. . .) inside a cell, just like a formula, and run Python scripts right inside your workbook. No need to leave Excel. No need to copy data back and forth.

This opens up a powerful new hybrid: Excel for structure, Python for logic and automation.

Python isn't going anywhere. It remains the most important language in finance for analytics, modeling, and automation. But now, you don't need to learn Python in the traditional sense. You need to learn how to use AI to write it for you—and where to use it to accelerate your work.

The Four Levels of Analytics—Powered by AI

To make better financial decisions, you need to make better sense of data. That sounds obvious, but most finance teams still spend a disproportionate amount of their time collecting, cleaning, and formatting data, rather than interpreting or acting on it.

The promise of AI in finance isn't just faster analysis; it's *smarter decision-making*, built on deeper insight and stronger context.

To structure this idea, we'll use a framework that's become foundational in analytics: the four levels of analysis. These levels move from hindsight to foresight, from passive observation to proactive action:

1. Descriptive analytics: What happened?
2. Diagnostic analytics: Why did it happen?
3. Predictive analytics: What is likely to happen?
4. Prescriptive analytics: What should we do?

Each level builds on the last. Each requires better data and stronger reasoning. And now, with the help of AI, each one is more accessible, more automated, and more actionable than ever before.

Let's explore what each level means, and how AI transforms how we approach them.

Descriptive Analytics: What Happened?

This is the foundation of all financial analysis. Descriptive analytics tells the story of the past. It answers questions like these:

- What were total revenues last quarter?
- How did costs change by category?
- What was our earnings before interest, taxes, depreciation, and amortization margin by region?

This is the world of financial statements, variance reports, dashboards, and key performance indicators. It's the information you need to run a business and answer stakeholder questions about recent performance.

Traditionally, descriptive analytics required hours of spreadsheet work: exporting reports, cleaning up messy data, aligning categories, and creating pivot tables or visualizations. It's important work, but it's also highly repeatable and time-consuming.

AI changes that.

With tools like ChatGPT and Copilot, you can describe what kind of summary you want—and get Python or Excel formulas back instantly. With AI assistants embedded in Power BI, you can generate natural-language summaries of visualizations. With LLMs, you can paste in raw data and ask for a concise, bullet-pointed executive summary of key changes.

AI doesn't just help describe what happened—it does it in seconds. This frees up your time for the next layer of work: *understanding why* things changed.

Diagnostic Analytics: Why Did It Happen?

Descriptive analytics tells you what changed. Diagnostic analytics explains *why*.

This is where finance adds real value—identifying the drivers of variance, investigating anomalies, and helping leadership understand the mechanics behind the numbers. Questions here include the following:

- Why did gross margin fall in Q2?
- What's driving the increase in selling, general, and administrative expenses?
- Why did our actuals diverge so far from forecast?

With the right prompts, you can ask AI to investigate drivers of change in a dataset. For example, if you have a time series of sales and marketing spend, AI can identify lagged correlations or segment behavior by region or customer type. If you provide transactional data, AI can help surface outliers, break down changes by category, and flag issues worth further investigation.

Even more powerfully, AI can *explain* the results. Instead of just returning rows of analysis, it can write a narrative: "The drop in margin was driven primarily by a 12% increase in raw material costs, partially offset by pricing actions in two of five regions."

That's the level of insight executives want—and AI helps finance teams deliver it faster, more clearly, and more consistently.

Predictive Analytics: What Is Likely to Happen?

Once you know what happened and why, the next natural question is, What comes next?

This is the domain of predictive analytics. It's where ML models begin to shine. Here, we shift from backward-looking analysis to forward-looking projections, using historical patterns to estimate future outcomes.

Common predictive use cases in finance include the following:

- Forecasting revenue or demand
- Projecting cash flow based on past trends

- Predicting budget overruns or cost spikes
- Identifying at-risk customers or contracts

Historically, predictive analytics was the domain of data scientists. Models had to be built, trained, validated, and deployed. But with AI—particularly with LLMs that can write Python for you—this step is now within reach for finance teams.

You can prompt ChatGPT with "Create a Python script using Prophet to forecast sales for the next six months based on this time series."

It will write the model for you. You can run it in Google Colab. You'll see the forecast with confidence intervals. You can modify the assumptions on the fly. And with enough iteration, you can embed this forecast into your reporting process—without having a background in statistics.

This is where AI starts to feel less like a tool and more like a teammate.

Prescriptive Analytics: What Should We Do?

Finally, we reach the highest level of analytics: prescription.

Prescriptive analytics doesn't just tell you what *might* happen—it recommends what you should *do* about it. It moves from insight to action. It's the kind of analysis that leads to prioritization, trade-offs, and decisions.

Examples:

- Given our cash flow forecast, how should we sequence our capital investments?
- Based on expected demand, what inventory levels should we hold?
- If revenue falls short by 5%, where can we cut cost with the least impact?
- Given multiple growth scenarios, which markets should we double down on?

This is the domain where scenario modeling, optimization algorithms, and decision frameworks come into play. And it's also where AI can help finance professionals become strategic advisors.

With LLMs, you can generate narrative scenarios—"What happens if our top three customers reduce spend by 10%?"—and get back not only numbers, but implications. With Python, you can simulate dozens of trade-off options and rank them based on net margin or return on capital. With AI tools, you can even build decision trees that incorporate both financial and nonfinancial inputs.

These four levels—descriptive, diagnostic, predictive, and prescriptive—will form the structure of this book.

Each one will get its own dedicated chapter. Each will include tools, prompts, use cases, and examples drawn from real finance work. As you move through them, you'll not only sharpen your technical skills—you'll change the way you think about what finance can do.

The Fast Pace of Change and the Need for Adaptability

One of the most disorienting aspects of working with AI today is how quickly everything moves. The models, tools, interfaces, and integrations that dominate the conversation one month may be outdated—or completely replaced—the next. What was considered cutting-edge six months ago might now be a baseline expectation.

Since the release of ChatGPT 3.5 in late 2022, the speed of evolution has been relentless. GPT-4o, Claude 2, Gemini 2.5, and countless open-source models have all entered the market within months of each other. Microsoft embedded Copilot into Excel, Word, and Teams. Google integrated AI into Gmail, Docs, and Sheets. Startups have flooded the space, each promising to automate, enhance, or revolutionize some aspect of how we work with numbers, language, or systems.

This rapid development can be both exciting and overwhelming. Just when you feel you've grasped how to use one tool, a newer, faster, smarter one emerges. As a finance professional, you don't have time to test every new platform, subscribe to every newsletter, or rewrite your workflows every quarter.

That's why this book isn't built on tools—it's built on *principles*.

What matters more than the name of the model is the thinking behind how to use it. What matters more than the specific AI assistant is how you approach prompting. What matters more than the syntax of one Python script is your ability to turn financial logic into an automated, repeatable process. Tools will change. The fundamentals won't.

This book teaches you how to think like a builder, a translator, and a strategist in a world increasingly shaped by intelligent systems.

To thrive in this space, you'll need a few key traits:

- **Adaptability:** The willingness to try, learn, and iterate quickly
- **Curiosity:** The instinct to explore how a tool might help you—even before you're told it will
- **Practical fluency:** Not in code or theory, but in how AI systems process language, solve problems, and interpret data

These are now leadership traits in finance.

We often talk about future-proofing skills. In the past, that meant staying current on International Financial Reporting Standards updates, mastering Excel shortcuts, or understanding regulatory shifts. Today, future proofing means being *fluid* in how you adopt and apply AI. It means not being locked into one way of doing things. It means approaching work with a mindset of "How can this be improved with automation or intelligence?" And increasingly, it means being able to guide others through this transformation—whether as a team lead, a trusted advisor, or a strategic partner to the business.

That's the real goal of this book: practical, tactical AI mastery for finance.

This is not an academic textbook. It's not a theoretical exploration of AI. It's a guide to *doing real work better*. You will learn how to do the following:

- Write prompts that get high-quality results from language models.
- Use AI to clean, analyze, and summarize financial data.
- Build basic forecasting models and automation flows with Python and no-code tools.
- Integrate AI into your planning, reporting, and decision-making processes.
- Think critically about when and how to use AI—not just to save time but to increase value.

And perhaps most important, this book will teach you how to lead in a new way.

Being AI-enabled isn't about knowing everything—it's about knowing what to ask, where to look, and how to experiment. The most effective professionals in this new era won't be the ones with all the answers. They'll be the ones asking better questions, iterating faster, and helping others see what's possible.

The chapters ahead will be practical, hands-on, and structured to reflect how real finance teams work. You'll be able to apply the ideas directly to your planning cycle, monthly close, or performance review process. Whether you're working solo or leading a global team, what you learn here will scale with you.

The next generation of finance isn't just digital. It's intelligent. And with the right mindset and skill set, you're ready to lead it.

Chapter 2

Prompt Engineering for Finance Professionals

When people first interact with a language model like ChatGPT or Microsoft Copilot, they often approach it like a Google search box. They type in a question or a request and hope for a complete answer in return. But unlike a search engine, which retrieves and ranks information, a language model is *generative*. It doesn't retrieve—it *produces*. And what it produces is entirely shaped by what you give it.

That input you type in? That's called a *prompt*. Understanding how prompts work is the foundation for using AI effectively in finance. If you know how to structure your inputs, you can get the model to write board commentary, summarize reports, generate

Python code, simulate scenarios, or even respond as if it were your chief financial officer (CFO).

But if you don't understand what's happening under the hood—even at a basic level—you'll find the experience inconsistent, confusing, and often frustrating.

This section explains how large language models (LLMs) read prompts, how they handle information, and what that means for how you should communicate with them.

What Is a Prompt, Really?

A *prompt* is any input you give to a language model. It can be a sentence, a question, a block of text, a table, a set of instructions, or a combination of all of those. It's your way of telling the model what you want it to do.

But more precisely, a prompt is *everything the model sees* before it responds. That includes not only your latest message, but also the context of the conversation so far—any background you've provided, previous instructions, and even its own past answers. This is important in finance workflows where conversations build over time.

For example, you might begin by pasting in revenue data, asking for a summary, then asking it to generate a slide title based on that summary. Every step is part of the evolving prompt.

So, when you think of a prompt, don't think of it as a single line of text. Think of it as a package of context that the model must read, understand, and act on.

How LLMs Read Your Inputs

LLMs like GPT-4, Claude, or Gemini don't read text the way you do. They break everything into small components called *tokens*.

A token might be a word, part of a word, or even just a few characters. For example, the word *forecasting* might be one token, but a number like 2024.75 might be split into two or three tokens depending on the model.

LLMs process these tokens in sequence and try to predict what comes next based on probability. For example, if the model sees the phrase "Revenue increased by 12% in Q2," it might predict the next sentence should mention reasons, implications, or next steps—because that's what it has seen most often in its training data.

The model doesn't understand your input like a human. It works through pattern recognition and probability across massive datasets. But because it has seen billions of examples of human writing—including business reports, financial statements, code snippets, and more—it can generate surprisingly useful and context-aware responses.

This is why clarity matters. If your prompt is vague or confusing, the model may not predict the next most helpful response. But if your prompt is structured, specific, and framed with the right language, you're far more likely to get a useful result.

What Are Tokens—and Why Do They Matter?

As mentioned, LLMs process inputs and outputs in tokens, not words. This matters for two reasons.

First, models have a token limit—a maximum number of tokens they can process at once. For example, GPT-3.5 can handle about 4,000 tokens per conversation; GPT-4 can handle up to 8,000 or 32,000 depending on the version. This limit includes both your input and the model's output. That means if you paste in a large financial report, ask for a detailed summary, and expect a long response, you may hit the token ceiling.

Second, tokenization can affect cost and speed. If you're using a paid API version of a model (such as GPT-4 through OpenAI's platform), you're billed by token. More tokens mean more cost and more processing time. For finance use cases, this is especially important when working with large data exports, month-end packs, or forecast simulations.

To manage this, do the following:

- Keep prompts concise but clear.
- Use summaries or aggregates rather than raw transactional data when possible.
- Ask for structured outputs to minimize back-and-forth.

Reasoning Models: How They Think

When we talk about LLMs thinking, we don't mean they understand context like a human. What they're doing is far more mathematical. These models use a neural network architecture—usually a transformer—that assigns weight to different words, phrases, and patterns based on how likely they are to follow what came before.

This process enables the model to simulate reasoning. It can walk through a calculation, compare trade-offs, or simulate a scenario. But all of that is the result of learned patterns, not actual comprehension.

Why does this matter in practice?

Because you can *guide* the model to reason more effectively by how you write your prompt. If you ask for "a five-point explanation of what's driving cost variance," the model knows to think sequentially. If you say "compare this month's numbers to last quarter and highlight risk areas," it will look for patterns of change. You are, in a sense, telling the model *how* to think—not just what to say.

Instruction Following Versus Completion-Based Prompts

There are two styles of prompting that affect how a model responds:

1. **Instruction following:** This is when you tell the model what to do directly:

"Summarize this P&L data in three bullet points."
"Write a paragraph explaining the variance in gross margin to the incorrect margin."
"Create a table comparing forecasted vs actual costs by category."

Instruction following is great for structured tasks. The model treats your request as a command.

2. **Completion-based:** This style is more open-ended and conversational. You start a sentence or pattern, and the model continues it:

"The revenue growth in Q2 was primarily due to . . ."
"In summary, we recommend the following actions: . . ."
"If actuals continue to trend above forecast, we should consider . . ."

Completion-based prompts can yield more natural or narrative responses, especially for commentary, storytelling, or simulations. They are also helpful when you want the model to think like you or mirror your writing style.

Both styles are useful in finance. Instruction following works well for reports, checklists, and scripts. Completion-based works well for messaging, commentary, or scenario analysis.

By understanding how prompts, tokens, and models interact, you're setting yourself up for success. You're no longer guessing what to say—you're guiding the model intelligently. This foundation will support everything that comes next, from prompting techniques to full financial planning and analysis (FP&A) workflows powered by AI.

Core Techniques Every Finance Professional Should Use

Now that you understand what prompts are and how language models interpret them, it's time to get practical. The way you design a prompt determines the quality, accuracy, and usefulness of the response. In this section, we'll walk through some of the most effective prompt engineering techniques that finance professionals can apply immediately.

Each technique will include a clear explanation, why it works, and how to use it in your day-to-day financial work—from reporting and commentary to automation and planning.

1. Few-Shot Learning: Use Examples to Guide the Model

Few-shot learning is one of the most powerful ways to improve the precision of your prompt. The idea is simple: before asking the model to perform a task, show it a few examples of what good output looks like. Then ask it to replicate the same format or logic with new inputs.

Think of it like training an intern. Instead of just saying, "Write a monthly commentary," you give them last month's version and highlight what you liked. The AI works in the same way—it learns from the pattern.

Example:

Prompt:

"Here's an example of the commentary I want you to emulate:

Input:

Revenue = $12.4M, Forecast = $13M, Variance = -$600K

Output:

Revenue came in 4.6% below forecast, primarily due to slower-than-expected sales in EMEA and a delayed product launch.

Now generate a similar commentary for the following:

Revenue = $15.2M, Forecast = $14.5M, Variance = +$700K"

The output will be something like this:

"Revenue exceeded forecast by 4.8%, driven by strong performance in North America and higher-than-expected demand in our software division."

This technique is ideal when you want consistency in reporting, tone, or structure. It's also extremely effective for commentary, executive summaries, email responses, or PowerPoint slide bullets.

2. Chain-of-Thought Prompting: Have the Model Reason Step-by-Step

One of the most common pitfalls when using language models is assuming they'll always return the correct answer right away. But LLMs work best when they're *guided* to reason through a problem—especially when it involves math, logic, or multistep analysis.

That's where chain-of-thought prompting comes in. Instead of asking the model to jump straight to a final answer, you prompt it to think through the steps out loud. This makes the model more likely to follow a logical sequence and reduces hallucinations (when the model confidently makes up information) or oversights.

Example:

Prompt:

"Our gross margin dropped from 45% in Q1 to 38% in Q2. Walk through three potential drivers of this change, reasoning step-by-step. Then suggest which is most likely."

Then the output will be something like this:

"Step 1: A drop in gross margin can be caused by an increase in cost of goods sold. Let's assess if input costs changed significantly.

Step 2: If COGS remained constant, the margin drop may be due to price cuts or revenue mix.

Step 3: A third driver could be a change in production efficiency or overhead allocation.

Conclusion: Based on past quarters, an increase in raw material costs is the most likely driver."

This is especially valuable when you want the AI to simulate how a finance analyst or CFO might approach a problem—not just give you a surface-level response.

3. Include Context Information: Add Relevant Data, Assumptions, or Constraints

LLMs are not connected to your systems, your spreadsheets, or your business logic—unless you give them the necessary information. That's why adding context is one of the most important prompt techniques in finance.

You can give the model, for example:

- Key metrics or key performance indicators
- Recent business events
- Specific assumptions

- Defined rules or constraints
- Internal definitions or naming conventions

When you include this context *in the prompt*, the model can produce far more relevant, grounded, and actionable responses.

Example:

Prompt:

"Assume the following:

> Revenue increased due to a 10% price hike in March
> COGS rose because of new supplier contracts starting in Q2
> The sales team added five new reps in North America in April.

Now generate a variance commentary explaining Q2 P&L changes."

Then the output will be something like this:

"In Q2, revenue gains were primarily driven by the full-quarter impact of the March price increase and expanded sales coverage in North America. The corresponding rise in COGS reflects newly negotiated supplier contracts that went into effect this quarter."

This technique is a must when working with internal data, confidential assumptions, or custom definitions not found in public datasets. Context bridges the gap between a generic answer and one tailored to your business.

4. Split Complex Tasks into Simpler Components

One of the biggest mistakes people make when prompting is asking for too much at once. If your question includes multiple instructions, conflicting priorities, or nested logic, the model may get confused—or try to do everything poorly.

The fix? Break the task down.

Split complex questions into smaller, more manageable pieces. Then either (1) solve them step-by-step within the same prompt using subtasks or (2) handle each part in a separate interaction.

Example:

Instead of asking:

"Analyze our revenue, forecast cash flow, and generate a slide explaining the trends in one prompt."

Do this:

Step 1: "Summarize the revenue drivers for Q3 based on this table."

Step 2: "Now forecast Q4 cash flow using the trend from Q2 and Q3."

Step 3: "Based on those two outputs, write bullet points for a slide summarizing financial highlights."

The model will perform better on each subtask because it can focus. And you maintain control over the structure and quality of each step.

5. Ask for Explanations Before Answers

This is a simple but powerful tweak: when you want more reliable answers—especially for finance logic, strategic recommendations, or forecasting—ask the model to explain before concluding.

By thinking out loud, the model forces itself to reason more clearly. This often leads to better conclusions and fewer hallucinations.

Example:

Prompt:

"Walk through the logic of whether we should cut marketing spend next quarter, considering ROI, pipeline, and recent revenue growth. Then give your recommendation."

Then the output will be something like this:

"Marketing ROI last quarter was 5.2x, well above our benchmark of 3x. Pipeline coverage for Q4 is currently 1.4x, slightly below target. However, revenue has grown steadily over three quarters, suggesting that momentum is strong. Cutting spend now could risk slowing that growth.

Recommendation: Maintain current spend and reassess mid-quarter."

This mirrors how a real finance professional might reason through a trade-off. You're not just getting an answer—you're getting structured thinking, which is far more valuable when presenting to stakeholders.

6. Role Prompting: Ask the Model to Act as a CFO, Controller, or Analyst

One of the easiest ways to steer the tone, structure, and depth of a response is to assign a role to the model. This is called *role prompting*, and it works because LLMs have been trained on vast amounts of data written from many different professional perspectives.

When you say, "Act as a CFO," the model accesses writing patterns, strategic language, and decision-making logic that match that persona. It will frame its answer with more focus on risk, alignment to business objectives, and executive-level clarity. If you ask it to act like a junior analyst, it may be more data-heavy or operational.

Example:

Prompt:

"You are a CFO reviewing a Q2 financial performance pack. Write a summary to present to the board, focusing on strategic implications, risks, and key variances."

Then this is an example of how the output might look like:

"Q2 performance exceeded forecast by 3.8%, primarily due to accelerated software sales in North America. However, gross margin pressure from rising supplier costs continues and may require price adjustments in Q4. I recommend revisiting our pricing elasticity assumptions before the next forecast cycle."

You can vary roles as needed:

- "Act as a financial controller" → strong on compliance, accounting accuracy
- "Act as a senior FP&A manager" → strong on insights, narrative, business drivers
- "Act as a junior analyst" → strong on data detail, breakdowns, and visuals

Use this whenever tone or perspective matters—board decks, internal comms, or stakeholder Q&A.

7. Output Formatting Prompts: Request Tables, Bullets, JavaScript Object Notation (JSON), or Markdown

The way information is formatted affects how easily it can be used. Fortunately, AI models respond well to formatting instructions—if you ask clearly.

You can request responses in the following forms:

- Bullet points
- Tables (Markdown or Excel-style)
- JSON (for developers or automation tools)
- Numbered lists
- Headings and subheadings

This is especially useful in finance, where clarity, structure, and standardization are key.

Example:

Prompt:

"Summarize the variance between forecast and actuals for Q3 in a table with columns: Metric, Forecast, Actual, Variance, % Difference. Round to one decimal."

Output:

Metric	Forecast	Actual	Variance	% Difference
Revenue	$12.0M	$13.2M	+$1.2M	+10.0%
COGS	$7.5M	$8.1M	+$0.6M	+8.0%
Gross Profit	$4.5M	$5.1M	+$0.6M	+13.3%

You can also use formatting to fit downstream tasks:

- For slides → "Format this for PowerPoint with title + three bullet points."
- For automation → "Format this in JSON so I can use it in a script."
- For reports → "Use Markdown with bold headings and clean structure."

Clear formatting reduces manual rework and helps you slot AI-generated outputs directly into your workflow.

8. Iterative Questioning: Refine the Scope Like a Conversation

One of the biggest mindset shifts in working with AI is understanding that your first prompt doesn't have to be your final one. In fact, *iterating*—asking follow-up questions, refining scope, or clarifying constraints—is how the best outputs are usually created.

The key is to treat the model like a collaborator. Start simple, then refine. Use natural follow-ups like this:

- "Can you simplify that?"
- "Now group by region instead of product."
- "Can you add a recommendation section?"
- "What if we assume revenue drops by 5% in Q4?"

Example:

Initial prompt:
"Summarize this P&L and explain key movements."

Follow-up:
"Now add risk areas and what we should watch for next quarter."

Follow-up:
"Great. Turn this into three bullet points for the COO."

Each iteration builds on the last, and the model remembers the full context. You're shaping the result in real time—no need to restart with every new question.

This technique is especially powerful for the following:

- Commentary
- Strategy decks
- Budget narratives
- Ad hoc analyses

Iterative prompting leads to outputs that are sharper, more specific, and more aligned to your needs.

9. Avoid Ambiguity: Use Concrete Language, Numbers, and Time Frames

AI models are extremely sensitive to ambiguity. If your prompt is vague, subjective, or too open-ended, you'll get inconsistent or generic results.

That's why in finance, *precision is key*.

Instead of saying:
- "Give me a summary of the report."

Say:
- "Summarize the report in four bullet points, focusing on revenue drivers, cost trends, margin changes, and future risks. Use plain business language."

Or instead of:
- "Compare Q1 and Q2 performance."

Say:
- "Compare Q1 versus Q2 gross margin. Highlight % change and explain whether the difference was due to cost inflation, volume, or pricing."

Be specific about:

- **Time periods** ("Q2 2024 actuals versus Q1 forecast")
- **Metrics** ("EBITDA margin" versus just "profit")
- **Audience** ("for board versus for sales team")
- **Structure** ("write a five-point summary with one key risk at the end")

The more concrete your language, the more grounded the response.

10. Use Constraints and Guardrails: Tell the Model What Not to Do

We often focus on telling the model what we *want*, but sometimes the key to a better output is telling it what to *avoid*. This is called *using constraints or guardrails*, and it's extremely helpful in finance where accuracy, tone, and appropriateness matter.

You can instruct the model to do the following:

- Avoid making up numbers.
- Stick to facts you provide.
- Use only specific terminology.
- Keep responses within a word or character limit.
- Avoid unnecessary explanations.

Example:

Prompt:

"Write an executive summary of this variance report.

Constraints:

- Use only the data I've provided.
- Do not speculate or add external assumptions.
- Keep the response under 120 words."

Expected output:

"Revenue exceeded forecast by $1.2M, driven by strong performance in North America and improved pricing. COGS rose by $600K due to supplier costs. Net profit increased 11%. No material changes in SG&A or CAPEX. Cash position remains stable."

The result is tight, factual, and professional. No fluff. No fiction. Just what you asked for.

You can even go further:

- "Don't mention any departments by name."
- "Don't use technical accounting language."
- "Avoid repeating data already shown in the table."

Constraints are especially important when the output will be reviewed by senior stakeholders or incorporated into published materials.

Applying Prompting to FP&A Workflows

With these fundamentals of prompting and a toolbox of high-impact techniques, now it's time to apply those skills to the day-to-day work of FP&A. Whether you're building assumptions, writing commentary, preparing slides, or investigating variances, prompting can help you save time, think more clearly, and deliver higher-quality outputs.

This section explores how prompting fits into real FP&A workflows—from planning and reporting to analysis and storytelling. You'll see how to use AI to automate tasks, improve clarity, and accelerate your thinking—without losing control of the output.

Prompts for Planning: Building Assumptions and Asking What-If Questions

The planning process is full of moving parts—assumptions, scenarios, targets, and constraints. One of the most powerful applications of prompting in this stage is using AI to clarify your logic and stress test your assumptions.

You can use prompts to do the following:

- Draft planning assumptions based on trends.
- Rephrase your logic into clear business language.
- Simulate "what-if" scenarios.
- Identify risks or blind spots in your forecast.

Example: Building Planning Assumptions

Prompt:

"Based on a 12% YoY increase in sales in 2023, and early Q1 growth of 3.1%, write three planning assumptions for 2024 revenue. Use plain business language, and include potential risks."

Output:

1. **Sustained growth assumption:** Sales will grow by 8–10% in 2024, assuming continued customer retention and expansion in EMEA markets.
2. **Product launch boost:** New product launches in Q2 and Q4 are expected to contribute an incremental $1.5M in revenue.
3. **Risk factor:** Macroeconomic uncertainty in LATAM could suppress demand in key consumer segments."

You can also prompt the model to simulate changes:

Prompt:

"What if Q2 sales underperform by 15%? What is the expected impact on annual targets and which cost levers could be adjusted?"

This type of prompting helps you explore scenarios dynamically and communicate your assumptions more clearly to stakeholders.

Prompts for Reporting: Automating Performance Summaries and Variance Explanations

Monthly, quarterly, and year-end reporting cycles involve significant time investment. You're pulling numbers, formatting slides, writing narratives, and preparing for review meetings. Prompting helps automate the text-heavy components and quickly translate data into language.

You can use prompts to do the following:

- Write monthly summaries.
- Explain variances in plain language.
- Compare actuals versus forecast or year-over-year performance.
- Highlight risks and next steps.

Example: Variance Commentary

Prompt:

"Write a performance summary for Q2.

Inputs:

- Revenue: $14.8M
- Forecast: $13.5M
- Variance: +$1.3M
- Key driver: Higher volume in North America
- Cost of goods sold: Up 9% due to raw material inflation"

Output:

"Q2 revenue exceeded forecast by $1.3M, driven primarily by volume increases in North America. COGS rose by 9% due to raw material inflation, partially offsetting margin gains. Overall, the business remains ahead of plan with positive topline momentum, though cost pressures continue."

You can take it further:

Prompt:

"Now write that same summary for a PowerPoint slide—title + three bullet points."

Output:

"**Title:** Strong Revenue Growth Offset by Rising Input Costs

- Revenue beat forecast by $1.3M, led by North America
- COGS rose 9% due to inflation, pressuring margins
- Continued topline momentum despite cost headwinds

This helps speed up your reporting cycle, reduces manual writing, and ensures consistency across stakeholder communications."

Prompts for Analysis: Investigating Drivers and Surfacing Insights

FP&A professionals are constantly asked to explain the why behind the numbers. Prompting can help you explore drivers, segment impacts, and even propose next steps based on quantitative results.

You can use prompts to do the following:

- Break down a performance delta by region, category, or product.
- Surface early indicators or anomalies.
- Ask the model to identify top drivers.
- Simulate reasoning across business units.

Example: Investigating a Drop in Gross Margin

Prompt:

"Our gross margin declined from 42% in Q1 to 37% in Q2. We've seen increased logistics costs and a shift in revenue mix toward lower-margin SKUs. Walk through potential drivers and recommend what to investigate first."

Output:

"Three likely contributors to the margin decline:

1. **Logistics cost inflation:** Rising transportation costs may have compressed unit margins across all SKUs.
2. **Revenue mix shift:** A higher proportion of sales came from lower-margin SKUs in Q2, particularly in APAC.
3. **Volume leverage loss:** If volumes didn't scale with fixed production costs, margins could compress.

Recommended action: Analyze SKU-level contribution margin and isolate the effect of volume on overhead absorption."

This prompt structure forces the model to reason and guide your analysis like a senior analyst or FP&A manager would.

Using Prompts to Write Commentary, Emails, and Executive Summaries

Writing is one of the most time-consuming parts of FP&A work. Whether it's monthly business reviews, commentary for reports, or stakeholder emails, finance professionals are constantly translating numbers into language.

Prompting can help you do the following:

- Draft first versions of your commentary.
- Rephrase technical insights into plain English.
- Adjust tone for different audiences.
- Create polished email responses to stakeholder questions.

Example: Executive Summary

Prompt:

"Write a 100-word executive summary for our Q2 results. Keep it factual, highlight revenue, margin, and one key risk. Audience is CFO."

Output:

"Q2 revenue reached $14.8M, exceeding forecast by 9%, driven by strong North America sales. Gross margin declined from 42% to 37%, primarily due to raw material inflation and a shift toward lower-margin SKUs. Operating expenses remained within budget, with no major variances. The key risk for Q3 is sustained cost pressure from suppliers, which may require pricing action or further negotiation."

Prompting also helps write emails:

Prompt:

"Draft a response to this stakeholder question: 'Why is our APAC margin lower than expected?' Keep the response clear and professional."

Output:

"Thanks for your question. The lower-than-expected margin in APAC was primarily due to an increased share of promotional sales, which carry a lower unit contribution. Additionally, shipping costs in the region spiked in early May, impacting landed cost per unit. We are currently reviewing contract terms and adjusting regional pricing strategies to address this."

AI can't replace your insight—but it can speed up your writing and help you sound clear, concise, and professional under pressure.

From Prompt to PowerPoint: Using Structured Outputs for Storytelling

Every FP&A team lives in PowerPoint—whether it's a strategy review, board pack, or performance update. Prompting can help you create slide content faster and more consistently.

You can ask for the following outputs:

- Slide titles
- Bullet point summaries
- Chart captions
- Talking points
- Key messages by audience (CFO versus sales versus operations)

Example: Prompting for Slides

Prompt:

"Create content for a slide titled 'Q2 Financial Highlights.' Audience: CFO. Use no more than three bullet points."

Output:

- "Revenue exceeded forecast by 9%, driven by volume in North America.
- Margin declined five points due to mix and input cost inflation.
- Cash flow remains stable; inventory slightly elevated due to shipment delays."

Prompt:

"Now write a short verbal script for this slide."

Output:

"In Q2, we continued strong topline momentum, outperforming forecast by 9%. While margin declined due to mix and inflation, our cost actions are underway. Cash and working capital remain stable despite minor delays in outbound shipments."

From here, you can copy/paste into your deck or use it to guide your voiceover in a leadership meeting.

Iterating Your Way to Better Results

One of the biggest misconceptions about using AI tools like ChatGPT, Gemini, or Copilot is that the magic happens in a single, perfect prompt. You type in a request, hit enter, and get back a fully polished, professional result.

In reality, it rarely works like that.

Just like writing a financial model or preparing a board pack, good output is often the result of drafting, revising, and refining. You're shaping a response—nudging it closer to what you want with each iteration. The faster you accept that your first prompt is just a starting point, the faster you'll get to useful results.

Why Your First Prompt Is Rarely Your Best

Think of prompting like asking a question in a meeting. If you're too vague, you get vague answers. If you're too specific too soon, you might cut off discussion. If you ask five people the same question, you might get five different—but equally valid—responses.

Prompting works the same way.

Your first prompt is your initial framing of the task. It sets direction, but it's rarely perfect. As you read the response, you'll often notice the following:

- It misunderstood the format.
- It skipped part of the question.
- It got the math wrong.
- It hallucinated a source or invented a reason.
- It gave you too much or too little detail.

That's okay. Instead of restarting from scratch, iterate.

Iteration is what turns a generic prompt into a high-performing tool.

How to Refine a Prompt Based on Errors or Hallucinations

Sometimes the model gives you an answer that *sounds* good—but when you check it, you find logical flaws, inconsistent numbers, or incorrect business assumptions. As mentioned, these are known as *hallucinations*.

Other times, the model simply doesn't understand what you're asking—especially if your prompt is unclear, too complex, or missing context.

Here's how to refine:

1. **If the logic is wrong:**
   Prompt: "You said revenue rose by 12%, but the numbers show a 4% drop. Can you double-check the math?"
2. **If it invents data:**
   Prompt: "Do not make up figures. Use only the data I provided. Try again."
3. **If it missed part of your question:**
   Prompt: "You covered revenue and margin, but you didn't address cash flow. Add that to the summary."

4. **If the tone is off:**
   Prompt: "This is too informal. Rewrite for a board audience with professional language."

When in doubt, ask the model to explain *how* it got to its conclusion. That often reveals where it made the mistake—and gives you the insight to improve your next prompt.

Another insight is that sometimes it is better to start another conversation with the LLM in a new tab rather than continuing in one where the LLM is not doing what you are expecting it to help you with.

When to Clarify, Simplify, or Narrow Scope

Many failed prompts are just too ambitious. They ask the model to do five things at once or operate with fuzzy inputs.

Here's what often works better:

- Break a big task into smaller ones (just like in a financial analysis).
- Ask one clear question at a time.
- Use numbered steps or bullet points to guide the structure.
- Be specific about what *not* to do (e.g., "don't make assumptions beyond the data").

Example: Original Prompt

"Summarize the P&L, write commentary for the CEO, and suggest three cost-saving actions based on Q3 actuals versus forecast."

The model might give you a surface-level answer that doesn't fully satisfy any part of the request.

Better Approach: Split and Simplify

Step 1: "Summarize the key P&L variances in three bullet points."
Step 2: "Now write a one-paragraph CEO update based on that summary."
Step 3: "Suggest three realistic cost-saving options based on the drivers you mentioned."

Each step builds on the last. You're steering the model clearly, without overwhelming it.

Example Iterations: Evolving a Forecast Prompt from Simple to Strategic

Let's walk through a common finance use case: forecasting revenue for next quarter.

Iteration 1: Basic Prompt

"Forecast Q4 revenue based on Q1 to Q3 data."
Problem: The model has no data to work with unless you give it. It will either hallucinate or ask you to provide inputs.

Iteration 2: Add Context

"Here's the quarterly revenue data:

- Q1: $10.2M
- Q2: $11.0M
- Q3: $12.1M

Forecast Q4 revenue using the growth trend."

Improved result: Now the model might calculate a linear growth rate and apply it.

Iteration 3: Add Constraints and Business Insight

"Same data as before. Assume product prices stay flat, but volume increases by 3% due to seasonal demand. Estimate Q4 revenue. Round to nearest $100K and explain your logic."

Final result: You'll get a number ($12.5M, for example), plus an explanation of how it was derived.

This is where prompting becomes more than a technical skill—it becomes a thinking aid. You're structuring your assumptions, checking your logic, and pressure testing your numbers—all with an intelligent assistant.

Resetting the Conversation: When It's Better to Start Fresh

Sometimes, no matter how much you iterate, the model stays stuck. It misinterprets the original prompt, carries forward a misunderstanding, or introduces persistent errors.

Here's a trick most advanced users rely on: *Close that chat and start a new one.*

Language models are *contextual*. They carry forward history from earlier parts of the conversation. That can be helpful for continuity—but it also means that one early misunderstanding can poison every future response.

If things start going sideways, don't fight it. Open a clean tab, paste in your revised prompt, and give the model a fresh start.

You'll often be surprised how much better the answer is when the model isn't carrying prior baggage.

Try Three to Five Tabs: The Parallel Prompting Strategy

Here's another technique used by professionals who want quality and optionality: *Open three to five tabs and run the same prompt in each one.*

Because language models are probabilistic—not deterministic—they generate slightly different answers every time, even to the same prompt. If your task is critical (board commentary, final forecast, pricing recommendation), run it in parallel and compare results.

From there:

- Choose the best version.
- Merge insights from multiple outputs.
- Or combine the strongest elements into your own polished result.

This is a fast, efficient way to avoid overreliance on a single answer—and helps sharpen your critical thinking in the process.

Saving and Reusing High-Performing Prompts

Once you've iterated your way to a prompt that works well, don't lose it. Save it.

- Use case (e.g., "monthly margin commentary")
- Inputs needed
- Output format
- Best variations

Prompts are reusable intellectual property. Once refined, they can cut your work time in half—or more. And when shared across your team, they become a productivity multiplier.

Examples of prompts to save:

- "Generate variance explanations from revenue tables."
- "Write CEO-ready summaries of financial reports."

- "Simulate a scenario impact on EBITDA with two assumptions."
- "Generate slide-ready bullets from performance data."

The more you use and improve these, the more powerful they become. AI doesn't get tired—but it does work best when *you* provide the clarity.

Building a Repeatable Prompting System in Finance

Once you've mastered the art of prompting—refining questions, iterating for better results, and applying techniques across your workflows—the next step is to build a system. A prompting system helps you scale the value of AI across your role, your team, and your entire finance organization.

This system doesn't have to be complicated. It doesn't require expensive tools or major process changes. It's about building structure and consistency into how you work with AI. Just like you have models, templates, and playbooks for budgeting or reporting, you can now have them for prompting.

How to Create a Prompt Library

A prompt library is exactly what it sounds like: a curated set of prompts that work. It's where you store, organize, and refine the instructions you've developed and tested across your finance tasks.

This can start as a personal resource—a Google Doc, Excel file, Notion board, or even a dedicated folder inside your AI tool where you save your best prompts. But the value multiplies when it becomes a shared asset.

If you work in a company with a finance team, consider creating prompt libraries for the following categories:

- **FP&A:** Forecasting, variance explanations, presentation summaries

- **Controllership:** Journal entry automation, reconciliation prompts, policy drafting
- **Investor relations:** Prompt templates for Q&A prep, earnings call narratives
- **Finance transformation/analytics:** Prompt-to-Python templates, automation design
- **Business partnering:** Tailored prompts for commercial insight generation or stakeholder briefing

A prompt library can be built individually or collaboratively. Some of the most effective teams I've worked with hold monthly or quarterly prompt-share sessions—similar to code reviews or best practice roundtables—where team members present successful prompts, explain their use cases, and add them to the shared library.

What's powerful about a prompt library is that it captures not just technical input—but domain knowledge. Prompts encode how your business thinks and speaks about financial performance. As your organization learns, the prompts evolve, too.

Organizing Prompts by Function

To make your prompt library usable, it should be well organized. One of the most effective ways to do this is by functional area or workflow category. Think of it like organizing your Excel templates—not by file name, but by the type of work they support.

Here's a sample structure:

1. **Reporting**
   - Summarize monthly performance in bullet points.
   - Explain top three variances versus forecast.
   - Generate commentary for the P&L by region.
   - Draft PowerPoint slide bullets for financial highlights.

2. **Modeling and Forecasting**
   - Generate assumptions for revenue growth scenarios.
   - Create Python code to build a simple forecast model.
   - Simulate headcount and cost impact of 5% growth.
   - Summarize inputs for a rolling forecast deck.
3. **Commentary and Communication**
   - Write email summaries of financial performance.
   - Turn a variance explanation into a board-ready paragraph.
   - Rephrase financial language for nonfinance stakeholders.
   - Translate Excel data into narrative commentary.
4. **Automation and Tools**
   - Prompt to clean and format data with Python.
   - Generate SQL to pull specific data fields from a database.
   - Describe a workflow and get Python + Power Query steps.
   - Build a task automation script using n8n or Make.
5. **Strategy and Decision Support**
   - Analyze trade-offs between two CAPEX scenarios.
   - Generate a SWOT-style summary based on inputs.
   - Turn scenario analysis into a decision tree format.
   - Simulate financial implications of business expansion.

Within each category, prompts can be further labeled:

- Inputs required
- Output format
- Estimated time to run
- Who it's useful for (analyst, manager, director, etc.)

This level of structure helps new users find what they need and empowers senior users to scale their knowledge across teams.

Using Prompt Templates as Part of Your Finance Toolkit

Just like financial models, prompting works best with templates—tried-and-tested structures you can reuse and customize. Prompt templates act like reusable macros or text snippets. They give you a consistent starting point.

Here's an example of a prompt template for performance commentary:

> "Based on the following actuals versus forecast data, write a variance commentary for the [department/region] for [month/quarter].
> Focus on: [one to two business drivers].
> Avoid: technical accounting language.
> Output: no more than 120 words, use professional tone."

Each time, you can adjust the fields: plug in the new month, change the driver, adjust tone if the audience shifts.

Over time, you'll build prompt templates for the following:

- Month-end close
- Forecast updates
- Strategic reviews
- Stakeholder presentations
- Board prep
- CEO or CFO talking points

These become assets you rely on—just like templates for budgets or headcount planning.

Best Practices for Documenting, Sharing, and Improving Prompts as a Team

When prompting becomes a team capability, a few best practices can make all the difference:

1. **Include prompt + output examples:** A good library doesn't just show the prompt—it shows the result. This helps others quickly assess if it fits their use case.

2. **Version your prompts:** Just like models evolve, so do prompts. Keep track of what worked best and what improvements you made over time.
3. **Encourage prompt reviews:** Make prompt sharing part of your team's rhythm. Ask: "What's a prompt you used this month that saved you time or improved your output?"
4. **Store prompts centrally:** Whether it's in Notion, SharePoint, Google Drive, or your business intelligence tool's internal wiki, make sure your team has a single home base to find prompts.
5. **Tag prompts with use case and owner:** Who wrote the prompt? What was it used for? When is it best applied? This metadata helps people reuse and build with confidence.

When teams treat prompts as shared assets—not individual shortcuts—they create more consistent communication, reduce duplication, and increase overall quality.

Prompting as a New Professional Skill: Not a Trick, but a Capability

It's worth saying clearly: *prompting is not a magic trick.*

It's not a clever hack or temporary shortcut. It's a new way of working—and it will soon be an expected capability for finance professionals at every level.

Prompting is the following:

- How you turn your thinking into code without being a programmer
- How you write faster and communicate more clearly
- How you automate workflows without a developer
- How you build systems that respond to change in real time

Most important, prompting is a new *interface* between your finance knowledge and the tools that now power the modern office.

Like Excel before it, prompting will become part of how finance is done. The professionals who master it early will not only be faster and more efficient—they'll also be the ones shaping how their teams, departments, and businesses evolve.

If you're serious about scaling your value, prompting isn't optional. It's a core skill—one that's not going away.

Chapter 3

Teaching AI to Code— Without Being a Programmer

Why Python Changed My Finance Career—and Why You Don't Need to Learn It All

If there's one technical skill that has completely changed how I work in finance, it's Python.

When I first encountered Python, I was a graduate student pursuing a master's in finance with a focus in data science at Monash University in Australia. At that time, Python was just beginning to gain traction in finance circles, mostly among data scientists, quantitative analysts, and some automation-focused controllers.

In the broader finance community, however, almost no one was using it. In fact, most people I worked with in financial planning and analysis (FP&A), controllership, and operations had never even heard of it.

But I knew immediately that it was something different.

Python wasn't just a programming language—it was a new way of thinking about and solving problems. It enabled me to automate manual reporting processes, model scenarios with greater flexibility, and work with larger, messier datasets in a structured and repeatable way. I could replace entire workflows that had previously taken hours in Excel with a few lines of well-written Python code. More important, I could do things that Excel simply couldn't—like building forecast models, merging multiple data sources, and applying statistical logic with real rigor.

I didn't learn it overnight. In fact, the learning curve was steep. I spent months reading documentation, debugging scripts, trying things that didn't work, and experimenting late at night just to build something functional. It was frustrating at times, but it was worth it—because with every challenge I overcame, I felt like I was adding a superpower to my finance toolkit.

Over time, Python became part of how I thought as a finance professional. I stopped relying on manual workarounds and started designing systems. Instead of just responding to requests, I was building tools that could be reused across teams. My insights became faster, more scalable, and more accurate. Python didn't replace Excel—but it elevated what Excel could do, and it fundamentally changed the speed and quality of my work.

Still, I knew this path wouldn't work for everyone.

Most finance professionals aren't going to spend hundreds of hours learning syntax, debugging code, or figuring out how to use machine learning libraries. That kind of deep technical investment is unrealistic when you already have a full calendar, operational targets, and reporting deadlines. And frankly, it shouldn't be necessary.

Which brings us to now—and to the artificial intelligence (AI) revolution we're living through.

With tools like ChatGPT, Claude, Gemini, and Copilot, *you no longer need to learn Python in the traditional way.* You don't need to take online courses, memorize syntax, or install packages from scratch.

You simply need to learn how to describe what you want and let the AI write the code for you.

This is one of the most important shifts happening in finance right now. Today, the barrier to entry has been lowered so much that anyone—analysts, FP&A managers, controllers, chief financial officers (CFOs)—can harness the power of Python without writing it from scratch.

If you know what kind of output you want, where your data is stored, and how your data is structured, you can get high-quality, working Python code from AI in minutes.

And if the first version isn't perfect, you can refine it. You can ask follow-up questions. You can debug collaboratively—like working with a junior developer who never gets tired.

This shift is game changing for finance professionals, because it makes advanced automation and analytics possible without requiring deep technical skills. You no longer need to be fluent in Python. You just need to be fluent in *your business logic*—and learn how to describe it clearly to a model that can translate it into code.

Let's be clear about something: the power of Python hasn't changed. It's still the most valuable language in the world for data analysis, modeling, automation, and financial transformation. It's used by hedge funds, central banks, startups, and Fortune 500 finance teams alike. But now, the interface to that power has changed. And that's what this chapter is about.

You are not going to become a full-stack developer—and you don't need to.

What you *do* need to learn is how to collaborate with AI tools that can write and explain Python code for you. You need to know how to describe your intent clearly, provide the model with the necessary context, and test what it gives you. You need to understand what Python can do, even if you don't know exactly how it does it. And you need to develop a few habits that enable you to run, interpret, and refine code in tools like Google Colab, Python in Excel, or Visual Studio Code.

Once you get the hang of it, the process is incredibly empowering. You go from asking ChatGPT things like "What's the average revenue growth?" to "Generate a Python script that reads an Excel file, calculates revenue growth by quarter, and plots it using matplotlib." And just like that—you're operating at a different level.

Here's what's important to remember: *this is not about coding, it's about commanding.*

You are telling the machine what to do, not doing it yourself. That's the key mental shift. It's no different from how we learned Excel: we didn't start by memorizing formulas. We learned by asking questions, testing logic, and building progressively more complex models.

Now, Python is just one more layer in that same evolution. And AI is the interpreter that bridges your business knowledge with technical execution.

Throughout this chapter—and also through other examples in the rest of the book—I'll show you how to work with AI to generate Python code that fits your needs. I'll teach you a simple prompting technique to structure your requests. I'll point you to where and how to run your code. And I'll give you practical use cases for every layer of financial analytics—from cleaning data to forecasting, from building dashboards to automating workflows.

By the end of this chapter, you won't be learning Python the old way. You'll be using Python, powered by AI, in a way that fits your role, your pace, and your business.

It's the most powerful tool in finance today. And now it's in your hands.

The Prompting Technique for AI-Generated Python

Now that you understand *why* Python is such a powerful tool in finance—and how AI is changing how we access that power—it's time to get hands-on. In this section, I'll show you the exact prompting technique I use (and teach) to get reliable, working Python code from AI, even if you've never written a line of code yourself.

This approach is simple, repeatable, and highly effective. Once you've used it a few times, it will feel like second nature. Think of it like filling out a short form: you provide the model with a few key pieces of information, and it generates high-quality, useful code in response.

Let's break it down step-by-step.

Step 1: Tell the AI Where You're Running the Code

This might sound unnecessary, but it's actually one of the most important steps. Different coding environments (Google Colab, Python in Excel, VS Code, etc.) behave differently, and the AI needs to know which one you're using in order to tailor the code accordingly.

Here's how to phrase it:

- "I'm using **Google Colab** to run Python code."
- "This code will be executed in **Python in Excel** using the =PY() function."
- "I'm using **Visual Studio** and already have pandas installed."

If you skip this step, the model might give you code that tries to display charts in a web browser when you're in Excel—or suggest file handling that won't work in your setup.

Be clear. Be specific. And if you don't know which tool you're using, just say that—AI will often give you multiple format options to choose from.

Step 2: Clearly Describe the Action You Want the Code to Perform

This is the core of your prompt. You're not writing code—you're *describing what you want done*.

The easiest way to do this is to start your sentence with this:

"Generate Python code that . . ."

Here are some examples:

- "Generate Python code that reads an Excel file and filters for rows where 'Region' equals 'EMEA'."
- "Generate Python code that calculates the YoY growth for each product category."
- "Generate Python code that merges two dataframes on a common 'Date' column and creates a new column showing the difference between forecast and actual."

You don't need technical jargon. Just describe the task like you would to a colleague.

The more specific your action, the better the output. Don't worry if you don't know the Python terms for what you want to do—the AI does. Your job is to be clear.

Step 3: Tell the AI Where Your Data Is Stored

Next, you need to tell the AI what data you're working with—and where it lives.

Most common options:

- "My data is stored in a dataframe called df." (This is standard in pandas, the most common Python data library. This works best when using Python in Excel.)
- "I'm uploading an Excel file named financials_q2.xlsx with a sheet called Actuals into Google Colab located here <add file path>"
- "The data is already loaded into memory from a CSV file called financials_dataset.xlsx"

This helps the AI understand how to access your data and what syntax it should use to reference it.

If you're using Python in Excel, you might say this:

- "I'm referencing a table in Excel using xl() in the =PY() function."

If you're using Google Colab, you might say this:

- "Assume I've already uploaded the file and read it using pd.read_excel() into a dataframe named df."

Think of this like explaining to a junior analyst where to find the file before asking them to work with it.

Step 4: Show the AI What Your Data Looks Like

This step is optional—but incredibly powerful. Instead of giving the model your full dataset (which might be huge), just paste in a sample of what the data looks like: three to five column names and two to three sample rows. You can do this by copying the output of df.head() from Python or just typing it manually.

Example:

> Ready when you are.

```
Here's a small sample of my FP&A dataset so you can understand the structure and fields:

| Month   | Department | Revenue   | Operating_Expense | Headcount |
| ------- | ---------- | --------- | ----------------- | --------- |
| 2025-01 | Sales      | 1,250,000 | 420,000           | 18        |
| 2025-01 | Marketing  | 320,000   | 210,000           | 9         |
| 2025-01 | R&D        | 0         | 380,000           | 22        |
```

This helps the model do the following:

- Understand data types (numbers, dates, text).
- Use the correct column names.
- Avoid misinterpreting the structure.

If your dataset is more complex, show the part that's relevant to the task. For example, if you're calculating forecast variance, show only the Forecast and Actual columns.

You'll be surprised how much better the output is when the model can see the data, even in abbreviated form.

Step 5: Request Clear Output Formatting

Finally, ask the model to give you output in a format that's easy to understand and use. This is especially helpful when reviewing or learning from the code.

You might add the following:

- "Please include comments in the code to explain each step."
- "Return the result as a table."
- "Plot the result using matplotlib with clear labels and a title."
- "Explain the logic after the code in simple terms."

AI-generated code is a teaching tool as much as a productivity tool. You want output that helps you *understand* what's happening—especially if you plan to reuse or modify it.

Putting It All Together: Sample Prompt

Here's an example using all five steps.

Prompt

"I'm using Google Colab to run Python code.
Generate Python code that reads an Excel file called budget_forecast.xlsx, filters for rows where Quarter equals Q2, and calculates the variance between Actual and Forecast columns.
My data is in a dataframe called df, loaded from the sheet called Data.

Here's a sample of the data:

Please include comments in the code and print a summary table showing each department, actuals, forecast, and variance."

Follow-Up Prompt (Optional)

"Now turn this into a bar chart showing the variance by department."

A Final Word: Don't Be Afraid to Tweak

Your first version of a prompt may not produce perfect code. That's okay. Use iteration:

- If the output is too long or messy: say "simplify the code."
- If a step is missing: say "add filtering for only departments with variance > $100K."
- If you don't understand it: say "explain this code line by line."

Think of prompting as a dialogue. You're not submitting a form—you're having a conversation with an AI assistant who knows Python fluently and is ready to build with you.

Once you've used this technique a few times, you'll develop a library of prompts for your recurring finance workflows—and you'll find that tasks which used to take hours can now be done in minutes.

What Can Python Actually Do in Finance?

Now that you've learned how to prompt AI to write Python code for you, the next big question is, "What exactly can Python do in finance?"

This is the challenge for most finance professionals new to Python. It's not that you don't want to use it—it's that you don't know what to ask for. If you've never seen Python in action, it's hard to picture the kinds of problems it can solve or the workflows it can improve.

This section will help you build that mental model.

We'll walk through the most powerful Python libraries for finance and FP&A and explore practical, real-world use cases. You'll also learn the types of tasks that Python does *better, faster,* and *more reliably* than Excel. Once you understand what's possible, prompting AI to generate Python code becomes significantly easier—because now, you'll know what to ask for.

Python Is a Swiss Army Knife for Modern Finance

Think of Python as a toolbox, not a single tool. It can read data, clean data, analyze data, visualize results, run forecasts, automate reports, and even create dashboards and web apps. And unlike Excel, which can become fragile and overloaded with too many formulas or links, Python handles complexity with elegance.

Here are the core areas where Python shines in finance:

- Data handling and cleaning
- Time series forecasting
- Statistical analysis and machine learning
- Reporting and visualization
- Dashboard and app development
- Workflow automation

Let's look at the specific libraries that make these possible—and how to prompt AI to use them.

1. pandas and numpy—Your Data Workhorses

These two libraries form the backbone of any financial data analysis in Python.

- **pandas** is for handling structured data—similar to Excel tables. It lets you filter, merge, group, and reshape data with far more power and flexibility than Excel formulas.

- **numpy** supports mathematical operations—useful when dealing with arrays, numerical calculations, or optimizing performance.

Use Cases
- Clean up messy Excel exports.
- Merge actuals and forecasts from two sources.
- Calculate variance by department, product, or region.
- Aggregate key performance indicators over time or by category.
- Create rolling averages or trailing 12-month metrics.

Example Prompt

"Generate Python code that reads a CSV file of monthly revenue, groups it by region, and calculates YoY growth using pandas."

2. yfinance—for Market Data and Stock Analysis

The yfinance library allows you to pull stock prices, financial statements, and historical trading data directly from Yahoo Finance.

Use Cases
- Pull monthly stock price history for competitors.
- Analyze beta and volatility for risk modeling.
- Track portfolio performance over time.
- Fetch historical financials (revenue, earnings, etc.) for benchmarking.

Example Prompt

"Generate Python code using yfinance that downloads daily stock prices for AAPL and MSFT over the last year and plots the closing prices."

3. Prophet—Forecasting Without a PhD

Developed by Facebook (now Meta), Prophet is one of the most user-friendly forecasting libraries available. It's great for finance professionals who want to model trends and seasonality without deep statistical knowledge.

Use Cases
- Forecast revenue based on historical sales.
- Account for seasonality and holidays.
- Visualize forecast confidence intervals.
- Perform scenario analysis on future periods.

Example Prompt

"Write Python code using Prophet to forecast next six months of revenue based on monthly sales data in a dataframe called df, with columns 'Date' and 'Sales.'"

4. scikit-learn—for Predictive Models and Machine Learning

scikit-learn is a powerful library for building machine learning models. While not every finance task needs ML, there are many strategic areas where it's useful.

Use Cases
- Predict future cost overruns based on past patterns.
- Classify customers by risk, behavior, or likelihood to renew.
- Cluster similar departments or cost centers by spending profile.
- Run linear or logistic regression to understand drivers of revenue or margin.

Example Prompt

"Create a regression model using scikit-learn to predict next quarter's revenue based on variables like marketing spend, sales headcount, and historical performance."

5. matplotlib and seaborn—for Static Visualizations

These two libraries help you turn raw numbers into compelling visuals.

- matplotlib is the foundation for plotting in Python—great for line charts, bar charts, and scatterplots.
- seaborn builds on matplotlib and offers cleaner, more insightful visuals with less code.

Use Cases
- Build variance waterfall charts.
- Visualize trends, seasonality, or distributions.
- Create comparison plots across departments or time periods.
- Replace Excel charts with more professional, data-driven visuals.

Example Prompt

"Plot a line chart of revenue by month using matplotlib, with labels, a title, and a trendline."

6. plotly—for Interactive Dashboards

Unlike matplotlib or seaborn, plotly creates interactive charts that respond to user input. You can hover over data points, zoom, or filter in real time.

Use Cases
- Create FP&A dashboards that clients or executives can explore.
- Build charts for web or internal reporting portals.
- Enable stakeholders to toggle among departments, regions, or scenarios.

Example Prompt

"Use plotly to build an interactive bar chart showing actual versus forecast by product category."

7. streamlit and dash—Build Simple Apps

With streamlit and dash, you can turn your Python scripts into interactive web applications without needing to become a web developer.

Use Cases
- Share a forecasting tool with stakeholders.
- Build a self-serve scenario planning interface.
- Enable teams to input assumptions and see updated financial outputs.
- Publish a dashboard without relying on IT.

Example Prompt

"Generate Python code using Streamlit to let a user input expected Q4 growth % and return updated revenue and margin forecasts."

Automate Workflows with Python

Python isn't just about analysis—it's also about automation.

Use Cases
- Clean and combine monthly files.
- Refresh dashboards on a schedule.

- Email reports to stakeholders.
- Integrate with APIs to pull or push financial data.
- Generate scheduled reporting scripts.
- Write code that emails your CFO the latest dashboard.
- Build scripts that auto-clean budget files.

Example Prompt

"Create a Python script that reads a folder of Excel files, merges them into a single dataframe, removes empty rows, and saves the cleaned version."

What you've seen here is just the surface of what Python can do in finance—but it should already give you dozens of ideas. Whether you're in FP&A, controllership, financial operations, or transformation, there's a place for Python in your work.

And remember—you don't need to memorize the syntax for any of this. *Your job is to describe what you want.* The AI will write the code. Your role is to review, test, and refine it for your use case.

As you explore the use cases in the chapters ahead—from descriptive analytics to automation—you'll return to many of these libraries. Each one is a tool in your kit. And now that you know what they're capable of, you'll be better equipped to ask the AI for exactly what you need.

Tools to Run Python Without the IT Headache

At this point, you've learned how to prompt AI to write Python for you—and you now have a solid understanding of what Python can actually do in finance. But there's still one crucial question left: "Where do you run the code?"

For many finance professionals, this is where things get intimidating. You might be thinking the following:

"Do I need to install something?"
"Will I break my computer?"

"Do I need permission from the information technology (IT) team?"

"Is this going to mess with my Excel files?"

The good news: running Python today is easier than it's ever been—especially with tools designed for non-engineers.

You don't need a complex setup. You don't need a developer's environment. And you don't need to convince IT to give you special access (in most cases). In fact, you can start using Python today with tools that work right in your browser—or even inside Excel itself.

In this section, I'll walk you through three of the best options for finance professionals:

1. Google Colab
2. Python in Excel (Microsoft 365)
3. Visual Studio Code (VS Code)

Each of these has its own strengths. Depending on your comfort level, work environment, and use case, you can choose the one that fits best. Let's break them down.

1. Google Colab—Zero Setup, 100% Browser-Based

If you're just getting started, Google Colab is the easiest and fastest way to run Python code.

Colab (short for *Collaboratory*) is a free online platform built by Google that lets you write and run Python in your web browser—no installations, no configurations, no admin access required.

Think of it like a Google Docs version of a Python notebook.

Key Benefits
- No setup is required—just go to colab.research.google.com.
- Run Python code line-by-line.
- Share your notebook with colleagues (like a Google Doc).
- It's great for experiments, prototyping, and learning.

- It has built-in access to the most common Python libraries.
- You can upload Excel or CSV files directly into your session.

Use Cases for Finance
- Run forecasting models with Prophet or scikit-learn.
- Clean up messy data exports from your ERP or business intelligence tools.
- Test AI-generated code quickly and safely.
- Visualize trends using matplotlib or seaborn.
- Automate repetitive Excel workflows (and export results back to Excel).

How to Start
1. Visit https://colab.research.google.com.
2. Click "New Notebook."
3. In the first cell, paste the Python code generated by your AI tool.
4. Hit Shift+Enter to run.

You can even write prompts like this:

"Generate Python code that reads an Excel file and runs in Google Colab."

The model will handle all the file reading and imports for you.

2. Python in Excel—Native Integration, Familiar Environment

This is a game changer for finance professionals who live and breathe Excel.

Microsoft has officially launched Python in Excel—which means you can now write and run Python directly inside your spreadsheets, using the =PY() function, just like any other formula.

This opens the door to combining Excel's structure with Python's power:

- Advanced statistical calculations
- Time series forecasting
- Data cleaning and reshaping
- Powerful visualizations

Key Benefits
- No need to leave Excel—just use Python where you already work.
- Results appear right in the sheet, alongside your other formulas.
- It offers native integration with Excel tables and ranges.
- It uses a secure cloud-based Python runtime (no local installation needed).
- It's great for recurring models and reporting workflows.

Use Cases for Finance
- Build forecasting models right next to your P&L.
- Clean and reshape large datasets from systems or exports.
- Build Python-powered visualizations inside Excel.
- Replace complex nested formulas with simple Python scripts.
- Use Python to simulate scenarios or sensitivity analyses.

How to Start
1. Ensure you're using Microsoft 365 (with Python in Excel access enabled).
2. In a cell, type =PY("your Python code here").
3. Reference Excel data using the xl() function inside your Python code.
4. Run the formula just like any other cell.

As of October 2025, Python in Excel is rolling out gradually through Microsoft 365 subscriptions—so check your access or talk to IT if you don't see it yet.

3. Visual Studio Code (VS Code)—Full Control for Advanced Users

If you're looking to level up and work on more complex projects, VS Code is the most popular and powerful option.

It's a free code editor developed by Microsoft, widely used by developers and data analysts. While it's more advanced than Colab or Excel, it gives you full flexibility to do the following:

- Work with multiple files.
- Build modular automation scripts.
- Integrate with version control (like Git).
- Install any Python packages you need.
- Connect to databases and APIs.

Key Benefits
- Full Python development environment
- Ideal for recurring automation or complex models
- Extensible with thousands of plugins and integrations
- Great for team collaboration and long-term projects

Use Cases for Finance
- Build and maintain a Python-based financial reporting system.
- Automate file ingestion and transformation pipelines.
- Connect to a database and run queries with AI-generated SQL.
- Develop a Streamlit dashboard for department heads.
- Use AI inside VS Code to write and debug scripts (via GitHub Copilot).

How to Start
1. Download VS Code from https://code.visualstudio.com.
2. Install the Python extension.
3. Create a new .py file and paste in your code.
4. Run the file line-by-line or as a full script.

You can ask ChatGPT for help with setup by prompting:

"Explain how to install and run Python code in VS Code, step-by-step."

If you're regularly working with code, this is the environment where you'll feel most productive and scalable.

Here's a simple way to decide:

Use Case	Best Tool
I want to try AI-generated Python quickly, with no setup.	Google Colab
I want to stay inside Excel but gain Python's power.	Python in Excel
I want full control over scripts, automation, and dashboards.	VS Code

You can even mix and match. For example:

- Prototype your code in Google Colab.
- Move it to VS Code when it's stable.
- Embed results into Excel using export scripts.

The important thing is to start—you don't need a perfect setup, and you certainly don't need permission from anyone to experiment.

AI Can Help You Run the Code, Too

Remember: you can use AI not just to write Python—but to help you run it. If you're unsure about how to use Google Colab or Python in Excel, just ask:

"How do I upload an Excel file in Google Colab and read it into a dataframe?"

"How do I write a Python formula in Excel to calculate YoY growth?"

"What are the steps to run a Prophet forecast in VS Code?"

The AI will walk you through it step-by-step.
You're never stuck—you're supported.

Chapter 4

Descriptive Analytics—Let AI Do the Reporting

What Is Descriptive Analytics?

In a world of AI forecasts, machine learning predictions, and algorithmic decision-making, it's easy to overlook the humble but powerful first step in the analytics journey: descriptive analytics.

Descriptive analytics is about one simple question: "What happened?"

This is the foundation of everything we do in financial planning and analysis (FP&A). Before we model the future, we need to understand the past. Before we forecast the next quarter, we need to explain the last one. And before we give any kind of recommendation to leadership, we need to establish a shared understanding of performance—grounded in facts, context, and clarity.

In other words, no matter how advanced your analytics stack becomes, you will always start with descriptive insight. It's not optional. It's essential.

And yet—descriptive analytics is also one of the most time-consuming, manual, and under-optimized parts of the finance workflow. In most companies, FP&A teams still spend the bulk of their reporting cycle cleaning up spreadsheets, chasing last-minute data, formatting reports, and writing repetitive commentary by hand.

The process is slow. The value is buried. And the pressure to move faster only grows.

This is exactly where AI steps in.

Large language models (LLMs) like ChatGPT, Gemini, and Microsoft Copilot offer a new way to approach descriptive analytics:

- Faster summary writing
- Smart commentary generation
- Automated data clean-up and formatting
- Instant bullet points for slide decks
- Narrative explanations for Power business (BI) dashboards
- Email-ready language for variance explanations

AI doesn't just analyze data. It translates it—into language, into insights, into deliverables. And this makes descriptive reporting one of the easiest and most impactful places to start using AI in finance.

In this chapter, we'll explore why descriptive analytics still matters more than most teams realize, what the traditional workflow looks like (and why it's broken), and how AI unlocks new levels of speed, clarity, and consistency across your reporting process.

Descriptive Analytics Defined: The What, Not the Why

Descriptive analytics answers questions like these:

- What were actual revenues in Q2?
- How did costs change by category last month?
- What is our cash position today compared to last quarter?
- Which departments spent above budget?
- How many units were sold in each region?

It provides factual, historical summaries—no predictions, no guesses. It's about describing reality as it was.

Descriptive Analytics—Let AI Do the Reporting

The most common descriptive tools in finance are the following:

- Profit-and-loss (P&L) statements
- Variance reports
- Trend lines
- Key performance indicators (KPIs) over time
- Actuals versus budget summaries
- Tables, charts, and dashboards

The goal isn't to explain *why* something happened (that's diagnostic analytics), or *what will happen next* (that's predictive). It's simply to give a clear, trustworthy snapshot of performance—something the entire organization can align on.

This kind of insight is foundational. But getting to it? That's where things break down.

Why Descriptive Work Is Still So Time-Consuming

In theory, descriptive analytics sounds easy. After all, we're just summarizing the past.

In practice, it's one of the most painful, messy parts of the finance cycle.

Here's what a typical month-end might look like for a finance team:

- Wait for actuals to be finalized from accounting.
- Pull multiple data exports (enterprise resource planning [ERP], human resources information systems, customer relationship management, etc.).
- Clean inconsistent column names or missing values.
- Combine actuals, budget, and forecast files.
- Run manual checks for completeness or anomalies.
- Create pivot tables and update visuals.

- Write performance commentary from scratch.
- Paste results into PowerPoint decks and format.

Each of these steps introduces manual effort, opportunities for error, and delays. By the time the report is ready, the insights are already aging. And the worst part? The work is highly repeatable.

AI thrives in repeatable environments. If you've done something before—and if it follows a structure—AI can help you do it again, faster and better.

How Descriptive Analytics Feeds Strategic Finance

Some finance professionals dismiss descriptive analytics as "basic reporting." But that's a mistake. When done right, it forms the *narrative foundation* for all higher-level analytics.

Here's why it matters:

- **It builds trust:** Executives want clean, accurate snapshots of performance before they make decisions. If your descriptive layer is wrong or unclear, everything that follows is questioned.
- **It highlights focus areas:** When variances pop, when revenue drops, when margins shift, descriptive analytics raises the flag that something needs deeper analysis.
- **It creates alignment:** Teams from finance, operations, marketing, and sales all need a shared version of the truth. Descriptive summaries keep everyone grounded.
- **It reduces noise:** Good reporting turns thousands of rows into a few clean messages—what changed, by how much, and where to look next.

Put simply: *descriptive analytics creates the story backbone* that your recommendations, models, and strategies are built on. That's why it's worth doing well—and worth improving with AI.

AI Makes Descriptive Analytics 10× Faster and 10× Clearer

Here's where the shift happens.

Imagine this: You paste a table of actuals versus forecast into ChatGPT. You ask it to generate three bullet points summarizing performance for your board slide. It returns:

- "Revenue exceeded forecast by 6.2%, driven by strong Q2 performance in EMEA.
- SG&A came in 4.5% below budget, primarily due to hiring delays.
- Gross margin improved YoY, despite inflationary pressures on raw materials."

This takes 10 seconds. And it reads like something your manager might write.

Or this:

You have a comma-separated values (CSV) of monthly headcount by department. You ask the AI to calculate year-over-year (YoY) changes, highlight top three increases, and write a summary for the HR Business Partner.

- "Headcount increased 11% YoY, with the largest growth in R&D (+22 FTEs), Marketing (+18), and Customer Success (+15).
- Growth aligns with strategic investments in product and customer support.
- G&A remained flat YoY, reflecting cost control focus."

You didn't write a formula. You didn't open Excel. You just described what you wanted.

That's the power of descriptive AI.

It takes:

- Your raw data (or summaries)
- Your prompt
- Your intended audience

And it returns:

- Bullet points
- Paragraph summaries
- Email-ready responses
- Slide content
- Executive talking points

It can do this across any of these tools:

- Revenue tables
- Expense summaries
- KPI dashboards
- Trend charts
- P&L comparisons
- Balance sheet movements
- Headcount and productivity metrics

It's like having a smart junior analyst who never gets tired, never misses a deadline, and always writes in your preferred tone—ready to summarize whatever you give it.

Using AI to Generate Performance Summaries and Commentary

Most finance professionals don't struggle to interpret data—they struggle to keep up with the volume of reporting that requires interpretation. Every month, quarter, and year, there's a familiar rhythm: close the books, check the numbers, summarize what happened, write it up, and share it with stakeholders.

In many companies, this process is still manual and repetitive. An analyst pulls the latest actuals, compares them to forecast, builds a few pivot tables, and then stares at a blank screen trying to write "Revenue increased by X% due to Y." That same cycle plays out across different teams, regions, business units, and time periods.

The result? Hours of effort are spent translating numbers into language—commentary for slides, summaries for reports, and explanations for emails.

This is one of the clearest use cases for AI in finance.

LLMs can take structured inputs—like tables, charts, or data summaries—and generate written output at scale. When guided properly, they can produce commentary that is clear, factual, consistent, and aligned with your tone of voice. And they can do it in seconds.

Start with the Right Input

AI needs structure to work well. If you give it raw data dumps or open-ended instructions, the output will often be vague or unhelpful. But when you provide clear, structured inputs—like actual versus forecast tables, percentage variances, or headline metrics—the results improve significantly.

Here's a simple rule: The more clarity you give the model, the more clarity you'll get back.

Start by feeding in a clean table or bullet-point summary of your data. You don't need to show the full P&L—just the relevant sections for the question you're asking. If you're focusing on gross margin, provide the relevant numbers for revenue and cost of goods sold (COGS). If you're summarizing operating expenses, show actuals, forecast, and variance by category.

Example input:

"Actual versus Forecast – Q2 2024:
Revenue: $12.4M (Forecast: $11.8M) → +5.1%
COGS: $7.2M (Forecast: $6.9M) → +4.3%
Gross Margin: 41.9% (Forecast: 41.5%)
Operating Expenses: $3.8M (Forecast: $4.2M) → −9.5%
Net Income: $1.1M (Forecast: $0.6M) → +83.3%"

That input alone gives the model a strong foundation to generate commentary.

Prompting for Commentary: A Practical Example

Once you've structured your input, use a clear and direct prompt. Here's an example:

"Based on the following data, write a short performance summary for Q2 2024. Keep it under 100 words, written for a senior finance audience. Focus on revenue, cost, and margin drivers."

What you'll typically get back is something like this:

"In Q2 2024, revenue exceeded forecast by 5.1%, driven by stronger-than-expected sales performance. COGS also came in higher, but gross margin held above target at 41.9%. Operating expenses were 9.5% below forecast, reflecting continued cost discipline. Net income significantly outperformed expectations, closing at $1.1M versus a forecast of $0.6M."

This is exactly the kind of language you'd write—or want to write—for a monthly pack or board deck. The value here isn't just in saving time. It's in getting a consistent, well-structured output you can then refine or use directly.

Role Prompting: Framing the Voice

One of the most effective techniques for improving the quality and tone of AI-generated commentary is role prompting. This means telling the model to respond as if it were a specific person or professional.

For example:

- "Act as a finance analyst writing a performance summary for a monthly report."
- "Write this as if you were a CFO preparing a summary for the board."
- "Summarize this as an FP&A manager explaining results to the head of sales."

Each role creates a different tone and level of detail. The analyst might provide more data. The CFO might focus on risk and strategic positioning. The FP&A manager might translate results into actionable points.

Prompting for role helps tailor the output to your audience—without changing the numbers.

Asking for Structure: Bullets, Paragraphs, or Slides

AI is flexible in its output format, and you can control the result by asking for the following output:

- Bullet points
- A single paragraph
- A slide-ready summary
- An email-friendly message

Examples:

"Turn this into three bullet points suitable for a leadership presentation."

"Write a one-paragraph summary for a board deck."
"Generate commentary that can be pasted into a PowerPoint slide."
"Write a short email to the COO summarizing these results."

This ability to match format to context is one of the reasons AI is so useful in descriptive reporting. You don't have to rewrite the same information multiple times for different stakeholders—you can re-prompt the model with slight adjustments and generate tailored outputs in seconds.

Common Prompting Patterns for Reporting

Following are a few repeatable prompts you can use across your reporting cycles.

Basic Performance Summary
"Summarize the Q3 financial performance using the actual versus forecast table below. Highlight revenue, cost, and net income changes. Keep it under 100 words."

Slide-Ready Bullets
"Write three bullet points summarizing key movements for a PowerPoint slide. Focus on topline, expenses, and margin."

Executive Email
"Write a professional email from a finance manager to the COO explaining Q2 performance. Be concise and objective."

Commentary for Multiple Regions
"Compare performance across EMEA, APAC, and North America using the variance table. Highlight which region over- or underperformed and suggest one possible reason."

Headline Generation
"Generate a headline for this performance summary suitable for a board deck."

This type of prompting isn't just useful—it's scalable. Once you develop your own prompt library, you can reuse and adapt these across business units, time periods, and reporting cycles.

Improving Accuracy: Grounding the Model with Data

To reduce errors or hallucinations, give the AI a clear rule: "Only use the numbers provided below. Do not guess or assume."

This helps keep the model grounded. While LLMs are trained on general knowledge, they don't know your business context unless you provide it. By giving it the data *and* the rules, you get more consistent and accurate results.

You can also add constraints:

- "Limit the summary to three key points."
- "Avoid using technical accounting terms."
- "Focus only on revenue and margin—not expenses."

These small adjustments lead to cleaner, more relevant commentary that aligns with your reporting standards.

When to Edit and When to Regenerate

Not every AI-generated summary will be perfect. Sometimes the tone won't fit. Sometimes it will state the obvious. Sometimes it may miss a nuance you'd catch instantly.

When this happens, you have two options:

1. Edit the output manually.
2. Prompt the AI to improve or rewrite it.

Examples:

- "Rewrite this in a more formal tone."
- "Make this sound more concise and avoid repetition."

- "Focus less on numbers and more on the business explanation."
- "Explain the impact on profitability, not just revenue."

This feedback loop makes the process faster with each cycle. Over time, you'll develop your own prompting patterns—and the outputs will require less editing.

Writing commentary is a cognitive bottleneck in finance. It's not that it's hard—it's that it's slow, repetitive, and constant. Every reporting cycle requires the same mental effort to describe what changed, how it changed, and why it matters.

AI doesn't replace your thinking—it scales it. It takes the structure you've already built (data tables, variance logic, report templates) and helps you express the insights faster, more clearly, and with less fatigue.

Automating Descriptive Reporting with Python, Excel, and Power BI

As you've seen in the previous section, prompting AI to generate commentary from financial results can save time, improve clarity, and create consistency across reporting cycles. But what happens when you pair this narrative generation with automated data processing?

You move from manual monthly reporting to a scalable reporting engine.

That's the power of combining:

- Python—for data transformation, calculations, and summaries
- Excel—for structure, familiarity, and now native AI capabilities
- Power BI—for dynamic dashboards, live data, and visual storytelling

These tools already exist inside many finance teams. But the workflows are often disconnected: data is pulled manually, cleaned manually, summarized manually, and copied from one tool to another. The process works—but it doesn't scale. It burns time, risks errors, and consumes valuable energy that could be spent on strategic tasks.

AI changes this.

By integrating automation with prompting, finance professionals can shift descriptive reporting from something they do manually to something they manage strategically.

In this section, we'll explore how to use Python, Excel, and Power BI—each with the support of AI—to automate the generation of descriptive analytics. The focus isn't on technical complexity. It's on practical workflows you can apply immediately.

Start with Python: Automate the Numbers

Python is an ideal foundation for automating descriptive reporting. It's fast, flexible, and well-suited for handling structured data like the kind you work with in FP&A—Excel exports, CSVs, ERP data pulls, or consolidated reports.

Even if you don't write Python yourself, AI can generate scripts for you, as covered in Chapter 3. Let's look at how that plays out for descriptive tasks.

Example: Automating a Variance Table

Imagine you receive monthly actuals and forecast data from your ERP system. You want to do the following:

- Merge both datasets.
- Calculate absolute and percentage variance.
- Flag any variances greater than 10%.
- Output a clean, readable table.

Here's what you can prompt:

> "Generate Python code that reads two Excel files—actuals_q3.xlsx and forecast_q3.xlsx. Both have a 'Department' column and a 'Revenue' column. Merge them, calculate variance in dollars

and percentage, and output the result as a new Excel file called variance_summary.xlsx. Include comments in the code."

The script might use pandas to read the files, perform the merge and calculations, and export the result—all in under 10 lines of code.

You now have a repeatable process: drop in your updated files each month, run the script, and get a refreshed variance report with no manual effort.

If you want more control, prompt AI to do the following:

- Add conditional formatting.
- Round values.
- Sort by largest variance.
- Include date or version stamps.

You're not just automating math—you're building a clean, standardized input that can then be fed into AI for commentary or directly into Excel or Power BI for visualization.

Excel: Familiar, But Now Enhanced

Most finance professionals are deeply comfortable in Excel. It's where budgets are built, forecasts live, and models are shared. And for descriptive analytics, Excel still plays a central role.

What's changed is that Excel is no longer limited to formulas and pivot tables. With tools like Python in Excel, Copilot in Microsoft 365, and Power Query, Excel is now a hub for automation.

Use Case 1: Python in Excel

Python is now integrated directly into Excel via the =PY() function. This allows you to run Python code inside your spreadsheet—on your data, in real time.

Example:

This replaces complex formulas with more readable, testable logic. You can run summary statistics, group data, or apply formatting rules directly using Python—without leaving Excel.

You can prompt AI to write these formulas:

> "Generate Python in Excel code to calculate gross margin percentage from columns B (Revenue) and C (COGS)."

Use Case 2: Power Query for Transformation

Power Query is Excel's built-in ETL (extract, transform, load) tool. You can automate data cleanup, unpivoting, column renaming, and much more. And with AI, you can now generate Power Query M code with simple prompts.

Prompt example:

"Write Power Query code to remove blank rows, convert 'Date' to proper format, and filter out values where 'Status' is 'Closed.'"

This is a powerful way to turn messy exports into structured, analysis-ready inputs—without building formulas by hand.

Use Case 3: Copilot for Commentary and Formatting

With Microsoft 365 Copilot, you can ask Excel directly to do the following:

- Explain a trend.
- Generate commentary.
- Suggest formatting.
- Build visualizations.

Prompt examples:

- "Summarize what changed between this month and last month."
- "Highlight rows where variance exceeds 10%."
- "Explain this chart in a sentence."

While still evolving, Copilot is bringing natural language interaction into Excel—turning it into a more intelligent reporting tool.

Power BI: Dynamic Reporting with AI Support

Power BI is a powerful platform for building dashboards and self-service reports. When used correctly, it becomes the front end for your descriptive analytics—letting stakeholders explore data without needing access to raw files or spreadsheets.

Where Power BI has historically focused on visuals, it's now incorporating AI-based insights into its interface, especially with Copilot in Power BI.

Use Case 1: Smart Narrative Visuals

Power BI includes a visual called Smart Narrative, which automatically generates a written summary of the chart or table it's connected to. You can use it to add commentary directly on the dashboard—no manual writing required.

You can also customize the narrative using DAX formulas or prompt-based templates.

Use Case 2: Q&A with Natural Language

Power BI supports Q&A visuals, where users can type natural language questions like these:

- "What was the total revenue in Q2?"
- "Show me variance by region over time."
- "List top five departments by cost increase."

The model interprets the question, queries the dataset, and returns a chart or table—live and interactive.

As a finance professional, you can use this to do the following:

- Explore your own data faster.
- Build interactive dashboards that support executive self-service.
- Pair charts with AI-generated commentary for a complete view.

Use Case 3: Copilot in Power BI (Emerging)

With Copilot, Power BI is moving toward a model where you can build reports with prompts:

- "Create a trend chart of monthly EBITDA."
- "Add commentary explaining the largest variance this quarter."
- "Build a visual comparing budget vs actual by department."

This reduces the technical barrier and enables you to focus on the insights, not the mechanics of report building.

End-to-End Workflow: From Data to Commentary

Let's tie it all together. Here's what a full AI-assisted descriptive analytics workflow might look like:

1. **Data Collection**
   - Export actuals and forecasts as Excel or CSV files.
   - Drop into a shared folder or automate via email/FTP.
2. **Data Processing (Python or Power Query)**
   - Use AI-generated Python or Power Query to clean, merge, and calculate metrics.
   - Export cleaned data to Excel or load into Power BI.
3. **Narrative Generation (LLM Prompting)**
   - Prompt AI to generate commentary from summary tables.
   - Tailor outputs for slides, emails, or dashboard captions.

4. **Delivery (Excel, Power BI, or PPT)**
   - Embed narratives alongside charts.
   - Use slide-ready prompts to create performance summaries.
   - Publish dashboards with automated insights.

This system doesn't require heavy engineering. You can build and manage it with the tools you already have. And once it's working, your role shifts from writing and formatting to reviewing and refining.

Turning Descriptive Outputs into Storytelling

Descriptive analytics answers the question "What happened?" But in a business setting, data alone is not enough. Even when the numbers are accurate and the tables are well-formatted, there's still a crucial step between raw insight and real impact: *communication*.

Stakeholders don't make decisions based on spreadsheets—they respond to narratives. They want clarity, not just completeness. They want key messages, not every metric. They want direction, not just detail.

This is where *storytelling* comes in.

As a finance professional, you're not just a source of data. You're a translator—connecting the numbers to the business context. And now, with AI's help, you can turn descriptive outputs into structured, stakeholder-ready stories in a fraction of the time it used to take.

In this section, we'll explore how to do the following:

- Use AI to shape descriptive commentary into narrative structure.
- Adapt outputs for different audiences (CFOs, sales leads, board members).
- Generate content for PowerPoint, dashboards, and executive emails.

Descriptive Analytics—Let AI Do the Reporting

- Build consistency across formats using structured prompting.
- Communicate clearly—even when you're summarizing complex or messy data.

This is not about adding drama or fluff. It's about making your insights easier to understand, faster to consume, and more aligned with what your stakeholders care about.

From Data to Message: Why Storytelling Matters

The shift from data to story is often invisible—but it determines whether your message is heard.

Let's take a simple example. You receive a monthly variance table for operating expenses:

Department	Actual	Forecast	Variance	%
Sales	1.2M	1.3M	−0.1M	−7.7%
Marketing	800K	900K	−100K	−11.1%
Finance	600K	580K	+20K	+3.4%

Technically, the data is all there. But without context, it leaves the audience to interpret it. Why was marketing under? Was that intentional or a risk? Why did finance go over?

When you add narrative structure, it becomes this:

"Operating expenses were 5.2% below forecast overall, driven by lower-than-expected spend in marketing and sales. Marketing underspend was linked to campaign delays, which are expected to resume next quarter. Finance exceeded budget slightly due to unexpected contractor costs related to system migration."

That's the insight. That's the story. And AI can help you generate this kind of messaging quickly and consistently.

Prompting for Storytelling: Structure over Style

To turn descriptive analytics into useful narratives, you don't need creativity—you need structure. AI is highly capable of generating structured outputs if your prompts give it the right scaffolding.

Here are a few structures you can use in your prompts:

1. Problem → Evidence → Implication
"Summarize this data by explaining what changed, why it changed, and what the business impact is."

2. Past → Present → Outlook
"Write a short summary of past performance, current status, and what we should watch going forward."

3. Metric → Driver → Recommendation
"Summarize each major metric, its main driver, and suggest one action we might take based on the data."

By embedding structure into your prompts, you avoid vague outputs and get commentary that reads like a finance professional wrote it.

Tailoring the Story to the Audience

One of the most valuable uses of AI in reporting is the ability to adapt the message based on who will read it. A CFO doesn't want the same details as a department manager. A board member doesn't want the same format as a business analyst.

AI can help you rewrite or reframe the same data for different audiences with simple prompting:

"Rewrite this summary for a CFO who wants a strategic view and a recommendation."

"Make this more operational—suitable for the head of marketing."

"Write this as an email to the board summarizing key variances."

You don't have to manually rewrite the same content five times. You can use a single source of truth, then ask AI to produce the right tone, length, and framing.

This increases your communication reach—without increasing your workload.

Generating Slide-Ready Content with AI

A large portion of finance reporting ends up in slide decks. Whether it's a monthly performance review, quarterly business review, or board pack, PowerPoint remains one of the most widely used formats for storytelling in finance.

Here's how to prompt AI to support your slide workflow.

Example prompt:

"Based on the table below, write a slide title and three bullet points for a Q2 financial performance slide. Focus on revenue, margin, and key risks."

You can also ask for:

- Short slide headlines
- Speaker notes for each slide
- Suggested chart captions
- Key takeaway summaries

You're not asking AI to design the slide—you're asking it to generate the content that you can paste into the slide. This saves time, improves consistency, and helps less experienced team members write at an executive level.

Dashboard Narratives: Closing the Loop on Visuals

Dashboards are increasingly common in finance reporting—especially in tools like Power BI or Tableau. But one thing dashboards often lack is interpretation. You can have beautiful visuals showing trends, variances, and performance metrics, but unless someone explains them, they can be misread or ignored.

AI can help you generate narrative captions that make dashboards more actionable.

Use this prompting strategy:

"Look at this table/chart and write a two-sentence summary explaining the main insight. Assume the viewer has no background context."

You can use this in these situations:

- Power BI Smart Narratives
- Dashboard footnotes
- Accompanying commentary sections
- Embedded tooltips for users

This layer of narrative transforms dashboards from static visuals to communicative tools. The AI doesn't guess—it uses the data you provide to state what happened, why, and what might come next.

Building Consistency Across Channels

Whether you're sharing results in Excel, PowerPoint, a dashboard, or an email, the message should remain consistent. AI can help standardize your language across all channels.

Example prompt flow:

1. "Write a one-paragraph summary of Q3 performance."
2. "Now turn that into bullet points for a slide."
3. "Now summarize those bullets into a sentence suitable for an executive dashboard."
4. "Write an email to the CFO using that summary and recommending one action."

Same data. Same logic. Four formats, each tailored to its context.

Without AI, this level of adaptability would require extra time and manual rewriting. With AI, you generate once and repurpose quickly—reducing risk of inconsistency and speeding up the reporting cycle.

Balancing Automation and Judgment

Storytelling in finance isn't about spinning a narrative—it's about clarifying meaning. AI can support this process, but your judgment still matters.

Use the model to do the following:

- Draft language.
- Highlight patterns.
- Propose phrasing.
- Suggest structure.

Then apply your expertise to these needs:

- Confirming accuracy
- Adjusting for nuance
- Aligning to strategy
- Adding contextual insight

Think of AI as your assistant—not your replacement. It drafts, and you refine.

Over time, you'll learn which prompts produce the best structure, what tone works for each stakeholder, and how to build a library of reusable narrative templates for your reporting cycles.

Final Thoughts

Descriptive analytics provides the foundation. Automation delivers the numbers. But it's storytelling that connects the insight to the action.

Finance teams that embrace this communication layer—supported by AI—will operate faster, with more clarity and more influence. The role of the analyst evolves from reporting numbers to guiding conversations.

And when AI helps you do the heavy lifting of writing, formatting, and translating metrics into messages, you get to focus on what matters: aligning your insights with business outcomes.

In Chapter 5, we'll move from *describing* the past to *understanding* it—entering the world of diagnostic analytics. You'll learn how to use AI not just to say what happened, but to explore *why* it happened. That's where the real leverage begins.

Chapter 5

From "What Happened?" to "Why Did It Happen?"

In finance, we're not just reporting what happened—we're expected to explain it.

Variance reporting alone isn't enough. Executives don't just want to know that gross margin declined. They want to understand *why*. Was it volume? Price? Input costs? Product mix? They want an explanation that's clear, credible, and actionable.

That's where diagnostic analytics comes in.

While descriptive analytics answers the question "What happened?," diagnostic analytics asks the next, deeper question "Why did it happen?"

This is the bridge between reporting and insight. It's where finance stops being a data delivery function and becomes a business partner. And today, with the help of artificial intelligence (AI) and Python, this level of analysis is not only more accessible—but significantly faster to produce.

In this section, we'll unpack the mindset of diagnostic thinking, show how to structure analysis using AI, and, most important, walk through how to prompt AI tools like ChatGPT or Gemini to generate Python code that surfaces root causes from financial data.

Why Diagnostic Analytics Matters

Month after month, FP&A teams produce reports that highlight variances—actual versus forecast, actual versus prior year, year-over-year (YoY) growth, month-over-month change, and so on.

But spotting a variance isn't the same as explaining it. Too often, variance tables end with a summary line that reads as follows:

"Revenue was 5% below forecast, primarily due to lower volumes."

That explanation might be true—but it's often based on intuition, not evidence. Or worse, it's based on anecdotal input from business partners. Diagnostic analytics gives us a framework to *verify* those assumptions using data.

The best finance teams don't just highlight deltas—they break them down:

- Which products contributed to the revenue drop?
- Was the variance driven by volume, price, or mix?
- Which regions or segments underperformed?
- Are there any underlying patterns or anomalies?

This kind of diagnostic clarity builds trust with leadership and helps prevent repeated surprises.

The Role of AI in Diagnostic Thinking

AI is not just a tool for answering questions. It's also a tool for *asking better questions*—and structuring your thinking.

With well-crafted prompts, AI can help you do the following:

- Generate hypotheses for variance drivers.
- Segment data for further investigation.
- Summarize findings by region, product, or customer.
- Suggest which variables may be influencing results.
- Translate raw data into causal narratives.

For example, you might provide a dataset showing actual versus forecast revenue by product and prompt the AI with this:

> "Based on this data, what are two to three potential explanations for the revenue shortfall in Q2?"

Or, with a bit more structure:

> "Act as an FP&A analyst. I'm providing a dataset with monthly revenue by product, including forecast and actuals. Write Python code that calculates the absolute and percentage variance by product, ranks the top contributors to the variance, and summarizes the top three drivers."

This approach combines prompting with Python—and gets you closer to a repeatable diagnostic process.

How to Prompt AI to Generate Diagnostic Python Code

Even if you're not a coder, you can use AI to generate Python that performs high-leverage diagnostic tasks. The key is to follow a structure—just like you would with descriptive prompts.

Here's a five-part framework for prompting AI to generate diagnostic Python code.

1. State the Environment

Tell the model where the code will run:

- Google Colab
- Python in Excel
- VS Code
- Jupyter Notebook

> "I'm using Google Colab to analyze financial data."

2. Describe the Dataset

Give a brief structure of your data (columns, a few sample rows).

3. Specify the Diagnostic Question

Focus on what you want the code to do:

- Calculate variance.
- Identify biggest contributors.
- Segment by region or product.
- Analyze volume versus price versus mix.

Example:

"Generate Python code to calculate variance between actual and forecast revenue, group the results by product, sort by largest negative variance, and print the top five contributors."

4. Ask for Interpretability

Request code comments and plain English output:

> "Add comments to explain each step. At the end, include a printout that summarizes the main drivers in a sentence or two."

5. Add Constraints (Optional)

If needed, you can add the following:

- Time filters ("just Q2")
- Regions or segments
- Sensitivity thresholds ("only show variance over 10%")

Diagnostic Thinking as a Mindset

More important than any code is the way of thinking that diagnostic analytics builds.

It encourages you to do the following:

- Ask why performance shifted—not just report that it did.
- Test assumptions instead of relying on surface explanations.
- Break performance into components (volume versus price, fixed versus variable costs).
- Segment your data to uncover hidden patterns.
- Move from symptoms to causes.

And when paired with AI, that thinking becomes faster, clearer, and more scalable.

Using AI to Surface Drivers and Ask Smarter Questions

As finance professionals, we're constantly under pressure to explain performance. Why did sales drop in Q2? What caused margins to shrink? Why did actuals come in over budget in one department but under in another?

Diagnostic analytics is about answering those questions with structure and evidence—not guesswork. But the reality is that many diagnostic exercises begin informally, with a manager asking, "What happened here?" followed by an analyst trying to find the pattern manually.

This is where AI can play a critical role—not by replacing judgment, but by helping you surface smarter questions and frame better analyses.

In this section, we'll explore how to use AI to do the following:

- Frame diagnostic questions clearly.
- Identify potential drivers or explanations.
- Generate code that segments or ranks data.
- Support hypothesis generation.
- Speed up your diagnostic process through structured prompting.

You'll learn how to treat AI like an analytical partner—one that thinks with you, not for you.

From Variance to Cause: Asking Smarter Questions with AI

The first step in any diagnostic process is recognizing that a variance exists. But the more important step is asking the right follow-up questions.

AI can help you structure those questions in ways that reveal insight. Instead of just asking "Why did margin drop?" you can ask questions such as these:

- Which cost categories increased more than expected?
- Was the decline consistent across regions or products?
- Did unit economics shift (e.g., lower volume or higher discounts)?
- Were there timing differences or nonrecurring items?

You don't need to know the answer to ask these questions—you just need to know what data is available and how to guide the model toward structured thinking.

Let's look at an example prompt:

"Act as a senior FP&A analyst. I'll provide actual and forecast data for revenue, COGS, and OpEx. Help me identify possible drivers of a 300 basis point decline in gross margin for Q2 2024. Focus on cost shifts, volume changes, or mix effects."

In this case, you're not asking the AI to guess. You're providing it with the input variables and asking it to *explore* possible explanations in a structured way.

Using Structured Prompts to Explore Drivers

Once you've identified a variance, your next task is to segment the data. This is where many diagnostic efforts go wrong. Teams often look at aggregate-level changes when the real story is hidden in subcomponents.

AI can help here—both in structuring your thinking and generating code or queries that do the segmentation for you.

Let's say you have a revenue shortfall. You can break down your prompt into diagnostic layers:

Level 1: Segment by Region
"Here's actual versus forecast revenue by region for Q2. Which regions contributed most to the shortfall?"

Level 2: Within Region, Segment by Product
"Within EMEA, break down the variance by product line. Which SKUs or categories underperformed?"

Level 3: Investigate Sales Drivers
"For the underperforming products, what might have driven lower sales? Was it volume, price, or order count?"

You don't need to code any of this by hand. Just describe your data structure and what you're trying to learn. The AI can suggest how to segment, what to calculate, and how to rank contributors.

From Observation to Hypothesis

AI is also effective at hypothesis generation—helping you move from pattern to explanation.

Let's say your expenses increased in one department by 15% over forecast. You can use this prompt:

> "Act as a finance business partner. I'm providing OpEx data by department. Help me generate three plausible explanations for a 15% increase in IT expenses versus forecast."

Or:

> "Here's headcount and labor cost data for the past six months. Write three hypotheses for why labor cost rose disproportionately last month."

These kinds of prompts don't give you final answers—they give you structured starting points. You can then use them to do the following:

- Guide conversations with business stakeholders.
- Shape your next round of data queries.
- Identify which variables to test or isolate.

AI won't know your business context better than you—but it can help you ask better questions and frame smarter starting points.

Combining Text Prompts and Code Generation

A powerful technique is to move fluidly between *text prompting* (asking AI for explanations or hypotheses) and *code prompting* (asking AI to generate Python for analysis).

Let's walk through an example:

Scenario

Your team has flagged a revenue shortfall in Q2 across several product lines.

Step 1: Start with a diagnostic text prompt:
"I'm investigating a $1.2M revenue shortfall in Q2. I have monthly actual vs forecast revenue data by product. Help me identify two to three ways to analyze which products contributed most to the variance."
AI may respond with the following:

- "Calculate absolute and percentage variance by product."
- "Rank products by total negative contribution to the variance."
- "Segment by product category to look for broader patterns."

Step 2: Move to a code prompt:
"Generate Python code to perform that analysis. My dataframe is called df, and it includes columns for Date, Product, Revenue_Actual, and Revenue_Forecast."
AI returns code using pandas to do the following:

- Group data by product.
- Calculate variance columns.
- Sort results and print top contributors.

Step 3: Prompt for interpretation:
"Based on the output, summarize the top three contributors to the shortfall in plain English."

This loop—data → prompt → code → summary—is the essence of AI-assisted diagnostic analytics. You're guiding the process, not just getting static answers.

Here are some diagnostic prompts for finance use cases.

Cost Overruns
"Here's monthly actual versus forecast data for cost centers. Identify which cost centers exceeded budget the most and suggest likely drivers."

Margin Compression
"Given revenue and COGS data by SKU, help me determine whether margin compression was caused by pricing pressure, input costs, or mix shift."

Revenue Miss
"Break down actual versus forecast revenue by customer segment and suggest where the shortfall originated. Include volume versus price if possible."

Headcount Variance
"Summarize which departments contributed most to the headcount variance versus plan and whether this impacted labor cost directly."

These are prompts you can reuse, adapt, and scale. They don't rely on AI being "right"—they rely on it helping you think better and faster.

Correlation, Clustering, and Attribution—With AI-Generated Python

Once you've framed the right questions and started exploring possible drivers of a variance, the next step is often to quantify those relationships. You don't just want to say "Marketing costs went up"—you want to understand *whether* and *how strongly* those costs are linked to revenue, margin, headcount, or other performance metrics.

That's where diagnostic techniques like correlation, clustering, and attribution analysis come in.

These methods help you move beyond speculation and into pattern discovery:

- **Correlation** shows relationships between variables (e.g., sales and marketing spend).
- **Clustering** groups similar data points to reveal hidden segments or behaviors.
- **Attribution** breaks down outcomes (like revenue or margin changes) into component drivers—such as volume, price, and mix.

In this section, we'll walk through each method in plain English, explain when to use it in a finance context, and—critically—show how to prompt AI to generate the Python code for you. No statistics degree required.

1. Correlation Analysis: Exploring Relationships

Correlation is one of the simplest and most useful statistical tools in diagnostics. It helps answer questions like these:

- Are marketing and sales moving together?
- Does headcount growth correlate with cost increases?
- Is customer retention related to support ticket volume?

The output of correlation analysis is a number between −1 and +1:

- +1 = perfect positive correlation (they rise and fall together)
- −1 = perfect negative correlation (one rises as the other falls)
- 0 = no correlation (they move independently)

Finance Use Cases

- Correlation between headcount and operating expenses (OpEx)
- Correlation between input prices and gross margin
- Correlation between region size and variance magnitude
- Correlation between customer tenure and revenue growth

Prompt Example

"I have a pandas dataframe with columns for Marketing_Spend, Sales_Revenue, and Customer_Churn. Generate Python code to calculate the correlation matrix between these variables, and visualize it as a heatmap using seaborn."

The AI will likely return a script that does the following:

- Calculates .corr() on your dataframe
- Uses seaborn.heatmap() to display the results
- Includes color-coding to show strength of relationship

Interpretation Tip

Correlation doesn't imply causation. But it helps you prioritize where to look more closely. If you see a high correlation between two variables, it may be worth exploring in more detail—or running a deeper regression analysis later.

2. Clustering: Segmenting Hidden Patterns

Clustering is a technique for finding natural groupings in your data. In a diagnostic setting, this is especially useful when you don't know in advance *how* things are different—but you suspect that not all products, customers, or business units are behaving the same.

Clustering helps you answer these questions:

- Which products behave similarly based on margin, volume, and growth?
- Can we segment cost centers by behavior or volatility?
- Are there groups of customers driving more frequent underperformance?

You don't need to define the segments in advance. The algorithm finds them based on similarity in the data.

Finance Use Cases

- Cluster products by financial performance (margin, revenue, volatility).
- Group customers by behavior (churn risk, value, frequency).
- Segment business units by budget adherence.
- Identify cost centers with similar growth or overrun patterns.

Prompt Example

"I'm using Python in Google Colab. My dataframe has columns for Product, Revenue, Gross_Margin, and YoY_Growth. Generate Python code using sklearn to apply KMeans clustering and group products into three clusters based on these metrics. Include a visualization of the clusters using a scatterplot."

AI will generate code that does the following:

- Scales the data
- Applies KMeans clustering
- Assigns cluster labels to each row
- Uses matplotlib or seaborn to plot the results

You can then use this prompt:

"Summarize the characteristics of each cluster based on the average metrics."

This helps you not just visualize the groups but also understand them in business terms.

3. Attribution Analysis: Breaking Down the Drivers

Attribution is one of the most valuable (and often underused) diagnostic tools in finance. It breaks down a change in a financial metric into component drivers.

For example, if revenue increased by $2M, was that due to which of the following?

- Higher *volume* sold?
- Higher *prices*?
- A change in *mix* (selling more of high-priced SKUs)?

This is often referred to as *price-volume-mix analysis,* and it's used frequently in FP&A, especially in revenue, margin, and cost diagnostics.

Finance Use Cases

- Revenue attribution: price versus volume versus mix
- Margin analysis: COGS changes by input category
- Headcount cost: full-time employee growth versus salary inflation versus contractor use
- Working capital shifts: days payable versus receivable vs inventory

Prompt Example

"I have a dataframe with actual and prior period data for revenue, volume, and average selling price by product. Generate Python code to perform a price-volume-mix analysis that breaks down total revenue change into:

- Revenue impact from volume change
- Revenue impact from price change
- Revenue impact from mix shift

Include comments in the code."

The AI will return code that does the following:

- Calculates total revenue for each period
- Computes the change due to each factor
- Summarizes the results as a breakdown

You can ask:

> "Add a final print statement explaining which factor had the biggest impact."
>
> This analysis transforms a generic statement like "revenue was up 8%" into:

- "5.2% was due to increased volume"
- "2.5% was from improved pricing"
- "0.3% was from a favorable product mix"

That's the level of clarity your stakeholders are looking for.

Combining These Techniques in Real Workflows

While these three techniques—correlation, clustering, and attribution—are powerful individually, they become even more useful when applied together in a diagnostic process.

Let's say you're investigating a gross margin decline. You might do the following:

1. Use correlation to check if input cost increases are linked to margin compression.
2. Use clustering to segment products or regions by performance.
3. Use attribution to break down the change into price, cost, and mix effects.

Each step uses different data and prompts, but AI can help you connect them. You can use this prompt:

> "Now that I've clustered the products into three groups, generate a separate price-volume-mix analysis for each group to see which segment is driving the margin pressure."

This layered analysis was once reserved for advanced analytics teams. Now, any finance professional who can describe the problem clearly can use AI to produce similar insights.

Tips for Prompting and Interpreting Diagnostic Models

- **Start small:** Ask for code that handles one part of the problem first (e.g., just correlation), then build from there.
- **Use sample data:** Even showing 5–10 rows helps the AI structure better code.
- **Ask for summaries:** After the code, prompt: "Write a plain-language summary of what this analysis shows."
- **Don't chase precision:** You're not building statistical models for academic papers—you're supporting decision-making.
- **Validate your intuition:** If AI shows a surprising correlation or pattern, explore it, but verify before drawing conclusions.

Building Repeatable Diagnostic Workflows

One of the most common problems in finance analytics is repetition without structure.

Every reporting cycle, finance teams revisit the same types of questions:

- Why did margin drop this quarter?
- Which cost centers exceeded budget?
- What explains the variance in headcount or revenue?

And each time, someone starts from scratch—manually pulling data, filtering spreadsheets, asking colleagues for input, and rewriting commentary. Even when the problems are similar month to month, the workflow isn't always repeatable.

Diagnostic analysis is often treated as an ad hoc task. But it doesn't have to be.

In this section, we'll walk through how to do the following:

- Create a repeatable system for diagnostic analytics.
- Use AI-generated prompts and scripts as reusable templates.
- Standardize the way you identify drivers, segment data, and explain results.

- Balance automation with human insight.
- Build a diagnostic playbook for your FP&A, controllership, or finance transformation team.

The goal is to make diagnosis part of your operating system—not a one-off effort triggered by a missed forecast.

Why Repeatability Matters in Diagnostics

You probably already have recurring descriptive reports: P&L statements, variance reports, dashboards. But how often do you have recurring *diagnostic* workflows?

If your team regularly investigates the same types of questions—margin shifts, revenue shortfalls, OpEx overruns—then creating reusable diagnostic components will save time and create consistency.

Benefits of repeatable diagnostics:

- Faster turnaround during close cycles
- More confidence in findings and summaries
- Less duplication across team members
- Easier onboarding of new analysts
- Greater analytical maturity across finance

Repeatability doesn't mean rigid. You're not automating conclusions—you're automating the process of investigation.

Step 1: Identify Your High-Value Diagnostic Patterns

Start by identifying the most frequent or impactful diagnostic questions your team deals with. These are your candidates for systemization.

For example:

- Gross margin diagnostics by product line
- OpEx variance analysis by department

- Price-volume-mix breakdowns for revenue
- Cost driver identification for controllable versus uncontrollable spend
- Forecast accuracy decomposition

These are not one-time analyses—they're recurring needs. Once you know your patterns, you can start building diagnostic templates based on them.

Step 2: Create a Diagnostic Prompt Library

Just like you might create templates for emails or reports, you can create a library of AI prompts for diagnostic use cases.

For each prompt, document the following information:

- The question it answers
- The structure of the input data required
- The AI prompt that generates the analysis
- An example of the expected output

Example Prompt Template: Price-Volume-Mix
Use Case: Decompose revenue variance by product
Input Needed: Dataframe with actual and forecasted volume, price, and product

Prompt:

"Generate Python code to perform a price-volume-mix analysis on this dataframe. Break down revenue change into effects from volume, price, and mix. Include explanatory comments in the code and a summary of the results."

You can build similar prompt templates for the following:

- Top five cost center overruns
- Clustering similar departments by expense behavior

- Revenue attribution by channel
- Correlation between external drivers and performance (e.g., foreign exchange [FX] rates, interest rates)

Store these prompts in a shared document or dashboard, organized by topic.

Step 3: Automate Where Possible, Customize Where Necessary

Once you have your prompt templates, the next step is to connect them to your workflow.

Let's say you have a monthly process where your team reviews margin changes by product. Instead of starting fresh each time, build a reusable script (via AI-generated Python) that can do the following:

- Ingest actual and forecast data.
- Calculate gross margin and variance.
- Segment by product or category.
- Highlight the largest contributors.
- Output a clean table for commentary.

Pair this with a prompt like this:

> "Write a paragraph summarizing the margin movement for the top three product lines that drove the change."

Now you have both the quantitative engine and the narrative overlay—ready to go each month.

If the business context changes, you can adapt it. But the structure stays consistent.

This is the ideal blend: repeatable structure, human judgment.

Step 4: Package Diagnostics into Playbooks

Take it a step further by building diagnostic playbooks for recurring scenarios.

A playbook is a simple document that poses these questions:

- What question are we trying to answer?
- What inputs do we need?
- What script or code do we run?
- What prompt do we use to get commentary?
- What should we watch out for in interpretation?

These playbooks can live in a shared folder, Notion, Confluence, SharePoint—any tool your team already uses.

Example: Margin Diagnostic Playbook

- **Trigger:** Margin dropped >200bps in a month or quarter
- **Inputs:** Revenue and COGS by product, volume, and price
- **Script:** AI-generated Python script for margin decomposition
- **Prompt for insight:**
  "Summarize the margin variance, identifying whether it was driven by pricing, input costs, or product mix."

- **Review Checklist:**
  - Are FX impacts included?
  - Were any SKUs discontinued or launched?
  - Are nonrecurring costs separated?

You don't have to build these all at once. Start with one or two high-impact workflows and build out over time.

Step 5: Embed Diagnostic Thinking into Team Habits

You don't need to make everyone a data scientist—but you can train your team to ask smarter diagnostic questions and use AI to structure their thinking.

Key practices to encourage:

- Always segment before you summarize. Don't just say "OpEx was over"—show by how much, where, and what changed.

- Always investigate before accepting assumptions. If a stakeholder says "Marketing costs were high because of the event," check the data.
- Always document the analysis. Whether it's a screenshot, code output, or commentary—show your logic.
- Always keep a record of prompts that worked well. Build your prompt library iteratively.

Encourage your team to use prompts like these:

"Help me identify the top three contributors to this variance."
"What might explain a drop in unit margin despite flat revenue?"
"Break this data into logical clusters for further review."
"Summarize this chart for an executive audience."
"Write a paragraph explaining this cost movement for a CFO."

Over time, this becomes muscle memory. Your team becomes not just faster—but more consistent, more insightful, and more aligned with the business.

Using AI Without Losing Ownership

A common concern with AI-driven analysis is losing control over the logic or relying too much on machine-generated summaries.

This is a valid concern—but easily addressed.

The goal is not to delegate responsibility to AI. It's to do this instead:

- Speed up the mechanical parts of the analysis.
- Help structure the investigation.
- Generate code that reflects your intent.
- Surface patterns you might overlook.
- Give you more time to apply judgment and context.

AI helps you move faster. But *you* are still the one interpreting results, refining assumptions, and presenting insights.

Think of it this way: if you had a junior analyst who could instantly code, summarize, and visualize—but needed your input to direct the analysis—you'd get more done. That's how AI should be used here.

Use Diagnostic Analysis Wisely with AI

Diagnostic analytics is a differentiator. It's what separates reporting functions from analytical finance teams. But for it to be sustainable, it needs to be structured.

With the right prompts, templates, and team habits, you can turn ad hoc diagnostics into repeatable workflows. You'll produce faster, better answers to the questions your organization keeps asking.

You don't need to build a full analytics platform. You just need the following:

- Clear diagnostic use cases
- Structured AI prompts and scripts
- A shared library of methods
- Analysts who are empowered to explore, segment, and explain

In Chapter 6, we'll move from asking *why something happened* to asking *what will happen next*. You'll learn how to use AI for forecasting, modeling, and scenario generation—powered by the same principles of prompting, clarity, and real-world application.

Chapter 6

Predictive Analytics

Forecasting in the Age of AI: From Intuition to Evidence

Forecasting is one of the most important—and frustrating—tasks in financial planning and analysis (FP&A).

Every month, quarter, or budget cycle, finance teams are asked to predict what's coming: revenue, costs, headcount, margin, cash. And every time, the process starts from the beginning. You pull the data, look at trends, talk to business partners, and build a model that tries to balance historical evidence with human judgment.

In many companies, forecasting still lives in Excel. Cells linked to cells. Assumptions hard-coded into formulas. Every update risks breaking something. And once the forecast is built, the real challenge begins: justifying it.

What if there were a better way to do this?

What if instead of manually constructing forecasts, you could describe what you wanted—and have artificial intelligence (AI) help you build the model? What if you could prompt the system to test scenarios, visualize trends, and even generate the Python code to automate the whole process?

This is not a future possibility. It's available now.

With large language models and Python's forecasting libraries, finance professionals can move from intuition-driven forecasting to evidence-based, repeatable, and transparent processes. You don't need to be a data scientist. You just need to know what you're trying to model—and how to describe it to AI.

In this section, we'll explore the following:

- The limitations of traditional forecasting
- How AI makes forecasting faster and more robust
- How to start prompting AI to write forecasting code for you
- What tools and libraries to use for simple, structured forecasting in Python

Let's start by looking at where most forecasting goes wrong.

The Problem with Traditional Forecasting in Finance

If you've spent time in FP&A, this scenario will feel familiar:

Your budget is locked. Your forecast is due. You're trying to update the revenue outlook. Sales gave you partial data, marketing hasn't sent their campaign assumptions, and the chief financial officer (CFO) wants to see three scenarios. You open your Excel model and start pulling in actuals, adjusting inputs, tweaking links, and hoping the formulas still work.

Most forecasting models in finance:

- Are built in spreadsheets with dozens of assumptions hidden across sheets
- Depend heavily on manual judgment and gut feel
- Use simple methods like straight-line projections or year-over-year (YoY) growth
- Are updated infrequently, even as conditions change
- Break easily when new products, cost centers, or data sources are introduced

The result? Inaccurate forecasts, limited transparency, and long cycles to build something that will likely be challenged in the next review meeting.

Forecasting doesn't need to be perfect. But it needs to be:

- Fast to update
- Transparent in logic
- Easy to iterate
- Built on evidence, not just opinion

That's where AI changes the game.

The Shift: From Manually Built to Prompt-Driven Forecasting

AI doesn't replace finance logic. It enhances it.

If you know what kind of forecast you want—monthly sales based on past trends, cost projections based on headcount, or cash flows linked to revenue and payment terms—AI can help you build the model.

Instead of writing formulas from scratch or coding from memory, you can prompt the model like this:

> "Generate Python code that forecasts monthly revenue based on the past 24 months of actuals. Use a simple linear trend and plot the next 6 months of forecast."

Or:

> "Create a forecast model where revenue = price × volume. Assume price grows by 2% quarterly and volume is projected by taking a three-month moving average. Generate the Python code."

You're describing what you want—not writing code.
That's the core idea behind AI-assisted forecasting.
And because these models are generated in Python, you gain access to much more flexibility:

- Automated trend and seasonality detection
- Scenario simulation with changing inputs
- Cleaner integration with data pipelines
- Easier reuse and scaling across time periods and teams

Let's look at the first building block: simple forecasting with Python and pandas.

Getting Started: Forecasting with Python Using AI

Before diving into advanced models, start with simple ones:

- Linear trend forecasts
- Moving averages
- Growth rate extrapolations

These can be built quickly using pandas and numpy—two foundational Python libraries for working with data.

Here's how to prompt AI to generate your first basic forecasting model.

Prompt Example: Linear Forecast Based on Historical Data

"I'm using Google Colab. I have a CSV file with monthly revenue data from Jan 2021 to Dec 2023 in a column called Revenue. Generate Python code to:

1. Load the file into a pandas dataframe.
2. Plot the historical data.
3. Fit a linear trend model.
4. Forecast the next six months.
5. Plot the forecast on the same chart as the historical data."

You'll get a complete script that can do the following:

- Load the data.
- Use numpy.polyfit() or a linear regression model.
- Create a forecast dataframe.
- Plot both actuals and forecast using matplotlib.

You didn't need to know the function names. You just described what you wanted.

If the output isn't quite right, you can refine your prompt:

"Add date formatting to the x-axis and label the forecast in a different color."

Prompt Example: Moving Average Forecast

"Generate Python code that calculates a three-month moving average forecast on historical revenue data. Use pandas. Extend the forecast for the next three months by repeating the last moving average value."

This creates a simple smoothing-based forecast—often good for short-term operational projections.

You can then build on this:

"Compare the moving average forecast with a linear forecast on the same chart."

Key Python Libraries to Know (and Prompt AI to Use)

You don't need to install or memorize these—but knowing their names helps you prompt effectively:

- **pandas**—For handling time series data, calculating moving averages, reshaping
- **numpy**—For numerical operations and fitting trend lines

- **matplotlib/seaborn**—For plotting actuals and forecasted values
- **statsmodels**—For regression and ARIMA models
- **prophet**—For advanced time series forecasting (covered in the next section)
- **scikit-learn**—For regression and machine learning-based forecasts

Example prompt to use these:

"Use statsmodels to fit an ARIMA model to monthly revenue data and forecast the next 12 months. Plot the forecast with 95% confidence intervals."

Or:

"Use Prophet to forecast monthly headcount growth based on historical HR data."

The AI will pull the appropriate syntax, install packages if needed, and comment the code.

Bridging Finance Logic and Statistical Models

AI works best when you provide business context alongside technical intent.

For example:

- "Revenue has grown steadily except in Decembers due to seasonality."
- "There was a major product launch in March 2023—exclude that from the trend."
- "Volume is stable, but pricing has increased by 3% YoY."

These details help AI adjust the model and ensure outputs match reality. You can even ask:

"Add a seasonality adjustment to reflect a 15% drop in December each year."

Or:

"Ignore outliers above the 95th percentile when fitting the model."

This isn't just code generation. It's business-driven modeling, guided by prompts.

Building Time Series Forecasts with Python and AI

Many forecasting challenges in finance involve time series data—metrics tracked at regular intervals, like revenue per month, expenses per quarter, or headcount by week. Unlike one-off assumptions or static models, time series forecasting uses historical patterns to project the future, taking into account trend, seasonality, and fluctuations over time.

Time series models are a natural fit for finance because they're built to answer exactly the kind of questions we're asked every day:

- What will revenue look like next quarter?
- How are costs trending across months?
- When will cash run out at the current burn rate?
- What does headcount growth look like for the rest of the year?

These forecasts don't need to be perfect. They need to be grounded, directional, and explainable.

And with AI's help, finance professionals can now build time series forecasts in Python without needing to write code from scratch or understand statistical theory.

In this section, you'll learn the following:

- What time series forecasting is and why it matters
- How to prompt AI to build models using Python
- Which libraries to use (Prophet, ARIMA, and others)
- How to structure your data for time series forecasting
- How to visualize, interpret, and refine the results

What Makes Time Series Forecasting Different?

Unlike models that treat each data point independently, time series models recognize that order matters. Each month's result depends in some way on what came before.

There are three major components time series models try to capture:

1. **Trend:** Is the data generally increasing or decreasing over time?
2. **Seasonality:** Are there recurring patterns at specific times (e.g., December dips, Q1 spikes)?
3. **Noise or irregularity:** Are there one-time events, volatility, or outliers?

In finance, nearly every major metric has some mix of these three. Sales might trend up, but dip every December. Expenses might spike in Q1 for annual licenses. Headcount might grow steadily but drop when contractors are offboarded.

Traditional Excel forecasting struggles with this complexity. AI-supported time series models handle it more naturally—if you know how to prompt for it.

Introducing the Prophet Library (fbprophet)

The easiest and most finance-friendly time series forecasting tool in Python is Prophet, developed by Meta (formerly Facebook). Prophet was designed to do the following:

- Handle business time series data (with irregular intervals, missing values, holidays).
- Model seasonality and trend automatically.
- Be usable by nonexperts with simple inputs.

It's ideal for FP&A professionals who want the following:

- Revenue forecasts based on historical sales
- Headcount projections
- Marketing ROI estimates over time
- Forecasts that account for holidays, promotions, or external events

Let's walk through how to ask AI to use Prophet to forecast finance data.

Prompt Example: Revenue Forecast Using Prophet

"I'm using Google Colab. I have a CSV file called monthly_revenue.csv with columns Date and Revenue. Generate Python code that

- Loads the data
- Prepares it for Prophet (renaming columns to ds and y)
- Fits a Prophet model
- Forecasts the next six months
- Plots actual and forecasted values
- Includes confidence intervals"

AI will generate a full working script, typically in 15–20 lines, that does the following:

- Imports Prophet
- Prepares your dataframe (df.rename(columns={'Date': 'ds', 'Revenue':'y'}))
- Fits the model with model.fit(df)
- Creates a future dataframe using model.make_future_ dataframe(periods=6, freq='M')
- Forecasts and plots the results with model.plot(forecast)

You can then extend the prompt:

"Add a table that shows the forecasted revenue for each of the next six months."

Or:

"Highlight any forecasted values that are more than 15% higher than the previous month."

Handling Seasonality and Holidays

Prophet includes built-in features for seasonality and holidays. You can prompt AI to include these in your model:

"Modify the previous code to add yearly seasonality and include US public holidays."

This will result in the following:

- .add_seasonality(name='yearly', period=365.25, fourier_order=10)
- .add_country_holidays(country_name='US')

You can also specify your own events:

"Add a custom holiday for Black Friday and model its effect on revenue."

This is especially useful for businesses with seasonal spikes around promotions, quarter ends, or industry events.

Using ARIMA with statsmodels for More Control

While Prophet is great for most finance use cases, sometimes you'll want more control or a different modeling approach. That's where ARIMA (AutoRegressive Integrated Moving Average) comes in.

ARIMA is better suited for these needs:

- Stationary time series (e.g., cost per unit, churn rates)
- High-frequency data (daily transactions)
- Data without strong seasonality

It requires more manual input—but with AI, you don't have to know the math.

Prompt Example: ARIMA Model Using statsmodels

"I have monthly expense data in a column called Expenses with a Date index. Generate Python code using statsmodels to do the following:

- Check if the data is stationary.
- Difference it if needed.
- Fit an ARIMA model.
- Forecast the next three months.
- Plot actuals and forecast together."

AI will walk through the following:

- Using adfuller test for stationarity
- Applying .diff() if needed

- Using ARIMA() from statsmodels.tsa.arima.model
- Forecasting and plotting the results

You can then prompt:

"Add AIC and BIC to evaluate model fit."

Or:

"Compare ARIMA and Prophet forecast outputs on the same chart."

This helps you select the best model for your data without deep statistical knowledge.

Visualizing the Forecasts

No matter which model you use, visualization is critical in finance. Stakeholders want to *see* the future, not just read about it.

Ask AI to do the following:

- Format plots clearly (with gridlines, labels, titles).
- Use different colors for actuals versus forecast.
- Show confidence intervals or forecast bands.
- Add vertical lines to mark today or important dates.

Example prompt:

"Improve the forecast chart by adding a vertical line to separate actuals from forecasted data, and use shaded areas for the confidence intervals."

With just a few tweaks, you can turn raw forecasts into stakeholder-ready visuals.

Structuring Your Data for Time Series Forecasting

For the model to work well, your data must be clean and structured. Minimum requirements:

- A date column in a consistent format (monthly, weekly, daily)
- A value column (e.g., Revenue, Cost, Headcount)
- No major missing periods (or explicitly handled with interpolation)
- Ideally, at least 12–24 time points (more is better)

You can ask AI to clean the data for you:

"Write Python code to fill missing months in a time series and interpolate revenue values."

Or:

"Filter the dataset to only include records from January 2020 onward."

You don't need to do this prep manually. Just describe the data problem, and AI can help fix it before modeling.

When to Use Prophet Versus ARIMA Versus Other Models

Situation	Best Tool
Clear seasonality and trends	Prophet
Short series, stable patterns	ARIMA
Driver-based forecast	Custom logic (pandas, numpy)
Complex regressions	scikit-learn
Multivariate time series	VAR (via statsmodels)
Business-facing dashboards	Prophet + plotly or streamlit

You can also ask AI:

"What model is best for forecasting monthly cash flow with strong seasonality and two major outliers?"

The model will guide you based on your situation.

Scenario Forecasting, Drivers, and Assumptions— Dynamic Planning with AI

Time series forecasting is a powerful way to extend historical trends into the future. But in real-world finance, you often need more than just a continuation of the past. You need to plan for what *could* happen.

That's where scenario forecasting comes in. Scenario forecasting is about modeling multiple possible futures—each based on different assumptions. It enables you to answer questions like these:

- What happens if prices drop 10%?
- What if we hire 20 new full-time equivalents next quarter?
- How would a slowdown in conversion rates affect revenue?

Instead of relying solely on statistical projections, scenario models let you simulate the impact of decisions, assumptions, and external events—and test how sensitive your business is to each one.

This section shows how to use AI to help you with the following:

- Building driver-based forecast models in Python
- Creating assumption-driven scenarios (best, base, worst case)
- Comparing scenarios visually
- Automating this process with AI-generated code

You don't need to write formulas by hand or know how to structure Python logic—AI will do the coding. You just need to clearly define your assumptions, structure your data, and guide the model with the right prompts.

From Time Series to Driver-Based Models

A driver-based forecast is built not from patterns in the past, but from your understanding of how the business works. These models reflect real relationships such as these:

Revenue = Volume × Price
Gross Profit = Revenue – COGS
COGS = Units Sold × Unit Cost
Labor Cost = Headcount × Average Salary

Driver-based models are useful in these times:

- Business conditions are changing rapidly.
- You want to simulate new products, channels, or teams.
- You need to explain *why* a forecast changed.

They're especially powerful when combined with AI and Python—because you can build complex models quickly, structure assumptions cleanly, and reuse the logic across scenarios.

Prompting AI to Build Driver-Based Forecasts

Let's start with a simple example.

You want to forecast revenue for the next six months based on these factors:

- Forecasted volume
- Assumed price growth
- A monthly conversion rate

Here's how to prompt AI:

"I'm using Python in Google Colab.
I want to build a revenue forecast based on:

- Volume (provided in a list for the next six months)
- Starting price of $50, increasing 2% per month
- Conversion rate of 85%

Generate Python code that:

1. Calculates price each month
2. Calculates revenue = volume × price × conversion
3. Outputs a dataframe with columns: Month, Volume, Price, Revenue
4. Plots the forecasted revenue over time."

You'll get clean Python code using pandas and matplotlib that does all of the requests.

From there, you can iterate:

- "Add a new scenario with 70% conversion."
- "Create a comparison chart between base and worst case."
- "Add commentary summarizing the differences."

Each new request can be added via prompting—no manual restructuring required.

Scenario Forecasting: Best, Base, Worst

A core principle of modern FP&A is planning for uncertainty. Instead of one forecast, you prepare multiple:

- **Base case**—your best estimate
- **Best case**—upside potential
- **Worst case**—downside risk

The goal isn't to be right—it's to be *prepared*.

AI can help you build and compare all three scenarios quickly.

Prompt Example

"Using the same driver-based model, generate three revenue forecasts:

- Base case: price grows 2%, volume is flat
- Best case: price grows 3%, volume increases 5%
- Worst case: price declines 2%, volume drops 10%

Plot all three forecasts on one chart with a legend."

The model will generate separate dataframes for each scenario, calculate revenue, and create a chart with clearly labeled lines for each case.

You can then prompt:

"Add a table that compares total revenue across all scenarios."

Or:

"Highlight in the chart where the worst case drops below $1M per month."

This is where AI and Python shine: scenario flexibility, built in minutes—not days.

Using AI to Build Flexible Assumption Inputs

One limitation of hard-coded models is that assumptions are buried in the logic. With Python and AI, you can make your model interactive and easy to update.

Prompt AI to structure your assumptions clearly:

```
# Assumptions
start_price = 50
price_growth = 0.02
volume = [1000, 1050, 1100, 1150, 1200, 1250]
conversion_rate = 0.85
```

Then use these variables throughout the code. You can change just one assumption to simulate a new scenario.

You can also ask:

"Create a function that takes price, volume, and conversion rate as inputs and returns forecasted revenue for six months."

This modular approach lets you reuse and adapt your forecasting logic across different models.

Scenario Comparison Charts and Dashboards

One of the most powerful outputs of scenario forecasting is a clear visual comparison.

Ask AI to do the following:

- Plot multiple lines on one chart (best, base, worst).
- Highlight the delta between base and worst.
- Shade the area between high and low scenarios (like confidence bands).
- Annotate inflection points (e.g., when cash runs below a threshold).

Example prompt:

"Create a line chart showing revenue over six months for three scenarios. Shade the area between worst and best case to show the forecast range. Label each line clearly."

You can go further:

"Add vertical lines for key planning dates (e.g., end of Q2)."

Or:

"Add data labels showing final month revenue for each scenario."

With a few extra lines, the chart becomes executive-ready.

Scenario Models with User Input (Streamlit or Excel)

Want to build something interactive?

Ask AI to generate a Streamlit app—a lightweight Python web app for input-driven models.

Prompt:

"Generate Python code using Streamlit that lets a user input volume, price growth %, and conversion rate using sliders. Based on these inputs, forecast sux-month revenue and display a line chart."

The result? A simple dashboard where users can test their own scenarios without touching the code.

Alternatively, prompt for Excel compatibility:

"Modify the forecast code to work with a CSV input file of assumptions and output the results as a new Excel file."

This is ideal for teams that want Python power but prefer to manage inputs in Excel.

Summary Table: What to Ask AI for in Scenario Modeling

Objective	Sample Prompt
Build base case model	"Forecast revenue from price × volume × conversion rate."
Add best/worst case scenarios	"Create three versions with different assumptions."
Plot comparisons	"Show all scenarios on one chart with labels."
Structure flexible assumptions	"Use variables for all inputs, not hardcoded values."
Make it interactive	"Build a Streamlit app for user-driven forecast modeling."
Export results	"Save forecast output to Excel with totals by scenario."

Forecast Evaluation and Continuous Learning

Building a forecast is only half the job. The other half is evaluating how well it performs—and using that feedback to make your future forecasts better.

This is a key part of predictive analytics that many finance teams overlook. Forecasts are created, shared, and then forgotten. But without checking how close they were to reality, there's no learning. And without learning, there's no improvement.

Modern forecasting is iterative. You build a forecast. You compare it to actuals. You measure the accuracy. You refine the assumptions, the drivers, or the model. Then you do it again.

The good news? AI can help you with every step of this process. In this section, you'll learn how to do the following:

- Use AI to calculate forecast accuracy.
- Prompt for code that compares actual versus forecast.
- Track errors over time (MAPE, RMSE, etc.).

- Improve your models based on performance.
- Build a simple feedback loop that makes your forecasts more reliable over time.

This is where forecasting becomes a true decision-support function—grounded in evidence and learning, not just intuition.

Why Forecast Evaluation Matters

Let's say your team forecasted revenue for the past six months. At the end of the period, actuals come in. You compare the totals and see you were off by 7%. Is that good? Bad? Where did the error come from?

If you don't quantify the accuracy of your forecast—and where it deviated—you're flying blind. You might do the following:

- Repeat bad assumptions.
- Trust a model that underperforms.
- Lose credibility with stakeholders.

The goal isn't perfection. It's consistency and transparency. If you're 4% off and improving over time, that's a win. But you can't improve what you don't measure.

The Most Common Forecast Accuracy Metrics

You don't need advanced statistics to evaluate your forecasts. Here are three simple and widely accepted metrics you can prompt AI to calculate for you:

Mean Absolute Error (MAE)
    Average of the absolute difference between forecast and actual. Easy to interpret (in original units).

Mean Absolute Percentage Error (MAPE)
    Same as MAE, but expressed as a percentage of actual. Easier to compare across departments or metrics.

Root Mean Squared Error (RMSE)

Emphasizes larger errors by squaring differences. Good for catching volatility.

Example Interpretation

- MAE of $250K = On average, forecasts were $250K off
- MAPE of 5% = Forecasts were off by 5% relative to actuals
- RMSE = Useful if large errors are especially damaging (e.g., cash flow)

Prompting AI to Calculate Forecast Accuracy

Let's say you have a dataframe with actuals and forecasts for revenue by month:

Month	Revenue_Actual	Revenue_Forecast
Jan	1,000,000	950,000
Feb	1,050,000	1,100,000

You can prompt:

"Generate Python code using pandas to calculate:

- MAE
- MAPE
- RMSE

between the actual and forecast revenue columns."

The AI will return code that gives you fast, clear feedback on how your model performed.

You can then prompt:

"Add a line chart showing actuals versus forecast for each month."

Or:

"Highlight the month with the highest forecast error."

Creating Forecast Accuracy Dashboards

With just a few more lines of code, you can turn evaluation into a dashboard:

- Bar chart of monthly errors
- Table of accuracy metrics by region or department
- Line plot of cumulative error over time

Prompt Example
   "Create a dashboard with three plots:

   1. Actual versus forecast revenue over time
   2. Monthly MAPE as a bar chart
   3. Cumulative forecast error as a line chart"

   These visuals help communicate to stakeholders:

- Where your forecast is strong
- Where assumptions broke down
- How confident to be in forward-looking models

Improving Forecasts with Feedback Loops

Once you've measured forecast accuracy, the next step is to ask these questions:

- Where were we most wrong?
- Why?
- What should we adjust next time?

This is where the learning happens.
Use AI to help you identify error patterns:

"Based on the forecast error by month, identify any seasonal or trend-based biases in the forecast model."

You can also prompt:

"Suggest improvements to the forecast model if MAPE exceeds 10% in three consecutive months."

AI might recommend the following:

- Adjusting assumptions (e.g., conversion rate too optimistic)
- Adding lag effects (e.g., leads convert slower than expected)
- Including seasonality or outlier adjustments

You can then prompt for updated code:

"Modify the existing forecast model to include a seasonality adjustment based on historical Q4 underperformance."

Or:

"Add a rolling three-month average as a smoothing layer to reduce volatility."

Each of these refinements builds toward a more robust, adaptive model.

Automating Forecast Evaluation and Updates

You can also prompt AI to help you automate this loop.
Example:

"Generate Python code that
1. Loads actuals and forecast data
2. Calculates MAPE

3. If MAPE > 10%, prints a warning and saves the error report to Excel
4. Otherwise, updates the model with the new data and saves the revised forecast."

This logic turns forecasting into a living system. Instead of a one-time build, it becomes a process that evaluates itself—and gets better each cycle.

You can also schedule this code to run monthly using tools like the following:

- Google Colab with scheduled notebooks
- Python scripts on a server or local machine
- n8n or Zapier for automation workflows
- Streamlit dashboards for interactive reporting

Communicating Forecast Confidence

Once you've evaluated the accuracy of your forecast, it's critical to communicate that confidence clearly.

AI can help you generate language for reporting:

> "Write a summary explaining that forecast accuracy for Q2 was within 4% of actuals, and that we expect similar performance in Q3 based on model refinements."

Or:

> "Draft a message to the CFO explaining that due to high volatility in input costs, forecast uncertainty remains elevated, and a wider scenario range is advised."

This helps build trust and shows that your forecasting process is not static—it's informed by results.

Final Thoughts on Forecasting with AI

Forecasting is not a set-it-and-forget-it exercise. It's a living process that improves through measurement, iteration, and refinement.

With AI, you now have the ability to do the following:

- Measure your forecast's performance in minutes.
- Diagnose what worked and what didn't.
- Adjust assumptions or logic through structured prompts.
- Build automated scripts that refine themselves over time.

This turns your role from being a spreadsheet forecaster to becoming a forecast architect—someone who manages the system, evaluates its output, and improves it over time.

In Chapter 7, we'll move from *predicting what will happen* to *recommending what should be done*. That's the domain of prescriptive analytics—and you'll learn how to use AI to simulate options, optimize decisions, and move finance from reporting to action.

Chapter 7

Prescriptive Analytics— From Insight to Action

From Forecasting to Decision-Making

By now, you've seen how artificial intelligence (AI) can help finance teams describe what happened (descriptive), investigate why it happened (diagnostic), and project what might happen next (predictive). But the most strategic layer is yet to come.

Prescriptive analytics answers a different kind of question: "Given everything we know, what should we do?"

It's the layer where insight becomes action. And for financial planning and analysis (FP&A) professionals, it's where the real value of AI can be unlocked.

What Is Prescriptive Analytics?

Prescriptive analytics goes beyond answering "what happened" or "what will happen"—it asks, "What's the best course of action, given the situation and constraints?"

In simple terms, it's the art and science of decision-making supported by data. It uses forecasting, assumptions, and business logic to simulate options and recommend the most effective path forward.

And while the term might sound technical, the reality is that finance professionals have been doing prescriptive thinking for decades:

- If revenue is soft, should we cut costs or invest in marketing?
- If headcount grows, what happens to payroll and benefits budgets?
- If product A is more profitable than B, how should we shift the mix?

The difference now is that with AI, we can model these trade-offs systematically—using code, data, and structured logic—not just opinion.

Why Prescriptive Analytics Matters in Finance

Finance professionals are increasingly expected to be business partners—not just reporters. That means moving from

"Here's the variance" → "Here's the forecast" → *"Here's what we should do."*

That last step is the most impactful. But it's also the most complex.

Prescriptive analytics brings clarity to decision-making. It helps answer questions like these:

- What's the most efficient way to allocate our budget?
- Which product mix will maximize gross profit?
- How can we reduce operating expenses (OpEx) without hurting key functions?
- What's the optimal headcount plan given our revenue targets?

And AI makes this kind of modeling faster, more accessible, and more repeatable.

The Building Blocks of Prescriptive Modeling

To move from forecasting to decision-making, you need to combine three ingredients:

1. **An objective**
   - What are you trying to maximize or minimize?
   - Examples: profit, cash, margin, efficiency, time, cost
2. **Decision variables**
   - What are the things you can control or change?
   - Examples: marketing spend, hiring plans, product mix, price levels
3. **Constraints**
   - What limits or rules do you have to respect?
   - Examples: budget caps, headcount limits, regulatory requirements, supply limits

In traditional finance, these models are often built manually in Excel with scenario toggles and circular references. But with AI and Python, you can describe the structure in natural language—and let the model generate the logic and code.

Prompting AI for Prescriptive Thinking

To begin using AI for prescriptive analytics, start by prompting it to suggest options, not just describe outcomes.
For example:

> "Act as a financial planning analyst. I'm trying to reduce our monthly OpEx by 8% without impacting revenue-generating functions. Suggest three strategies based on typical expense categories in tech companies."

Or:

> "We have a $2M budget and three initiatives: A (ROI = 120%), B (ROI = 80%), C (ROI = 150%). Recommend how to allocate funds to maximize total return, assuming partial funding is allowed."

In both examples, you're doing the following:

- Framing the objective (reduce OpEx, maximize ROI)
- Naming the variables (functions, initiatives)
- Imposing constraints (no revenue impact, budget limit)

These are the exact components of prescriptive models.

The Shift in Prompting Style

Up to now, you may have been prompting AI to do the following:

- Analyze data.
- Summarize results.
- Build forecasts.

Now you'll start prompting AI to do the following:

- Recommend actions.
- Simulate outcomes.
- Optimize results.
- Weigh trade-offs.

This requires a slightly different mindset. You're not just asking "what is?"—you're asking "what if?" and "what should?"

Here's an example that reflects that shift.

Descriptive Prompt

"Summarize monthly variance in marketing spend versus forecast."

Prescriptive Prompt

"Given that we are $200K over budget YTD in marketing, suggest three cost-reduction options that would bring us back on track without cutting campaign volume."

You're giving the model a business problem—not just a dataset.

Framing Decisions as If-Then Statements

One useful technique in prescriptive analytics is structuring your prompts as decision logic. You can describe outcomes as *if-then scenarios* and ask the model to help simulate or prioritize them.

Example:

"If we shift $100K from Product B to Product A, which has a higher margin, what is the projected impact on gross profit?"

Or:

"If we delay headcount growth by one quarter, how much OpEx do we defer?"

These kinds of prompts lead naturally into simulation or optimization, which we'll explore in the next sections.

But even before coding, AI can support you in framing the decision, asking smarter questions, and generating alternatives.

From Forecast Outputs to Action Inputs

If you've built a forecast in the previous chapters—especially scenario-based ones—you're ready for prescriptive action.

Let's say you forecast the following:

- Revenue will decline by 4% in Q2.
- Gross margin will fall from 42 to 39%.
- OpEx is trending flat.

You can now ask:

"What are three options to preserve operating margin in Q2 despite the revenue drop?"
Or:

"Assuming we want to maintain a 20% EBIT margin, what cost reductions are needed based on our current forecast?"
AI can help generate the following information:

- Decision options
- Quantified trade-offs
- Suggested sequencing (e.g., reduce marketing first, defer hiring second)

AI as a Decision-Making Assistant

Think of AI not as a calculator, but as a decision-making assistant. You describe the goal, the levers, and the limitations—and it helps you structure the analysis.

Prompt AI to do this:

- Lay out assumptions clearly.
- Present two to three alternatives.
- Highlight risks and side effects.
- Estimate rough business impact.
- Write a short recommendation summary.

Example:

"We are considering reducing our contractor budget by 15%. What risks should we consider, and what alternative options might deliver similar savings with less operational disruption?"
Or:

"Draft a slide that shows three cost optimization options, their estimated savings, and the pros/cons of each."

You're no longer just analyzing data—you're guiding decisions.

Prescriptive analytics is the final evolution of data-driven finance. It's where your role shifts from delivering reports and forecasts to enabling real business decisions. And with AI, you can now move through that evolution faster, more consistently, and with far less friction.

Now we'll go hands-on with optimization modeling using Python. You'll learn how to use AI to generate actual code that solves for the best solution given your financial goals and business limitations—bringing prescription to life through logic, math, and automation.

Using Optimization Models in Finance with AI and Python

One of the most powerful (and underused) techniques in finance is optimization. It's not just about building a forecast or scenario. Optimization is about choosing the *best* possible decision among many alternatives—based on your business goal and your constraints.

Optimization models enable finance teams to do the following:

- Allocate limited budgets across competing priorities.
- Decide the optimal product mix to maximize margin.
- Minimize costs while meeting operational requirements.
- Plan headcount while staying within budget caps.
- Choose between investment options under resource constraints.

Before AI, building these models required mathematical modeling and programming experience. But now, you can describe your objective and constraints in plain English, and AI will generate the Python code that builds and solves the model for you.

Let's start by defining the basics.

What Is an Optimization Problem?

Every optimization model has three components:

1. **Objective function**
   What are you trying to maximize or minimize?
   Examples: maximize profit, minimize cost, optimize utilization
2. **Decision variables**
   What are the things you can change or decide?
   Examples: marketing spend, number of units produced, headcount allocation
3. **Constraints**
   What limits or conditions must be respected?
   Examples: budget limits, minimum staffing levels, resource availability, time

These are already familiar ideas to anyone in finance. The difference now is that we can use AI to structure them into a working model that solves for the optimal solution.

Prompting AI to Build an Optimization Model

Let's say you have three departments (A, B, C) and a $1M budget to allocate. Each department has a known return on investment (ROI), and you want to distribute the funds to maximize total ROI.

Prompt:

"I want to allocate a $1M budget across three departments:

- Dept A (ROI = 120%)
- Dept B (ROI = 100%)
- Dept C (ROI = 80%)

Each department must receive at least $100K.
Generate Python code using PuLP to find the allocation that maximizes total ROI while respecting the budget and minimum funding constraints."

The model will return this:

- A definition of variables: how much to allocate to A, B, and C
- An objective function: maximize A×1.2 + B×1.0 + C×0.8
- Constraints:
  - A + B + C ≤ 1,000,000
  - A, B, C ≥ 100,000

It will use PuLP, a Python package for linear programming, to solve the problem and print the optimal allocation and total ROI.

Introducing PuLP: The Linear Programming Library

PuLP is a Python library designed for building and solving optimization problems. It supports the following:

- Maximization or minimization
- Linear constraints
- Variable bounds (e.g., minimum/maximum funding)
- Solver integrations (e.g., CBC, Gurobi)

You don't need to learn the syntax. Just describe your business problem, and AI will use PuLP to structure the model.

Example prompt:

"Use PuLP to decide the optimal mix of three products to manufacture, based on the following:

- Product A profit = $12/unit, max 200 units
- Product B profit = $9/unit, max 250 units
- Product C profit = $15/unit, max 150 units
- Total labor hours available = 1,000
- Product A takes 2 hours, B takes 1.5 hours, C takes 3 hours

Goal: maximize total profit."

This kind of optimization logic is difficult to do manually in Excel. With AI, it takes one prompt and produces repeatable, auditable logic.

Alternative Library: scipy.optimize for Simpler Problems

For simpler cases, AI might choose scipy.optimize, which is part of the broader SciPy ecosystem. It's great for these situations:

- Small-scale optimization problems
- Problems without strict equality constraints
- Scenarios where you don't need integer solutions (e.g., fractional outputs are okay)

Prompt example:

"Use scipy.optimize to minimize total shipping cost from three warehouses to four destinations, given cost per unit shipped and supply/demand constraints."

Unless you're doing more advanced or nonlinear optimization, PuLP is generally more intuitive and flexible for finance use cases, especially when the output must be whole numbers (e.g., headcount, units).

Use Case 1: Budget Allocation to Maximize Return

Problem: You have $5M to allocate across 5 business units with different ROIs and minimum funding needs.

Prompt:

"Use PuLP to allocate funds across Business Units A to E with these constraints:

- Minimum allocation: $500K each
- Max total: $5M
- ROIs: A = 1.1, B = 1.05, C = 1.15, D = 0.95, E = 1.2

Maximize total return."

AI will create the model, solve it, and tell you how much to invest in each business unit.

Use Case 2: Workforce Planning Under Constraints

Problem: You want to plan headcount across three regions to meet demand, stay within budget, and balance coverage.
Prompt:

"We have a headcount budget of $900K.
Region A cost per FTE = $100K, B = $90K, C = $110K
Each region must have at least five FTEs.
We want to maximize total coverage score: A = 1.0, B = 1.2, C = 0.9
Build an optimization model using PuLP."

This kind of prompt combines cost control, minimum staffing, and a weighted business goal—all solvable in minutes with AI-generated Python.

Use Case 3: Product Mix Optimization

Problem: Given labor and material constraints, which products should be prioritized for maximum margin?
Prompt:

"We have 2,000 hours of labor and 5,000 kg of material.
Product A: $20 profit, 2 hrs labor, 5 kg material
Product B: $15 profit, 1 hr labor, 3 kg material
Product C: $25 profit, 3 hrs labor, 7 kg material
Use PuLP to decide how many units of each product to produce to maximize profit."

This shows how AI can operationalize finance trade-offs—at scale, with clarity.

Interpreting Optimization Outputs

Once AI gives you the solution, you'll get this information:

- The optimal values for each decision variable (e.g., "Allocate $1.2M to B")
- The value of the objective function (e.g., "Total expected return: $5.6M")
- Whether constraints were binding (e.g., "Marketing maxed out budget")

You can ask follow-up questions:

"Which constraints were limiting our total return?"
"What would happen if we increased the budget by 10%?"
"Rerun the model assuming Business Unit D must receive $1M minimum."

This creates a fully *interactive decision model* that responds to leadership input in real time.

Visualization and Communication

Once you have the output, ask AI to visualize it:

- Bar chart of optimal allocation
- Comparison chart of scenarios
- Table summarizing ROI versus allocation

Prompt:

"Create a bar chart showing the optimal allocation by business unit, and annotate the total expected ROI."

You can then embed this into your slides or use AI to help generate this:

"Write a short summary for leadership explaining how the optimization model improved our budget allocation vs last cycle."

AI for Simulations and Scenario Recommendations

Prescriptive analytics doesn't always have to deliver one perfect answer. In many financial decisions, what we really want is to explore a range of possible futures, evaluate their likelihoods, and identify the most robust or risk-aware path forward.

This is where *simulation modeling* comes in.

Unlike optimization, which solves for the single best decision based on fixed inputs, simulation can do the following:

- **Explores variability:** It runs many scenarios with changing assumptions.
- **Quantifies risk:** It shows the distribution of outcomes, not just the average.
- **Supports resilience:** It helps finance teams plan for volatility, not just precision.

And with AI, building these simulations becomes dramatically easier.

What Is Monte Carlo Simulation?

Monte Carlo simulation is a technique that uses random sampling to model uncertainty. It runs thousands of variations of a model with different random inputs to see how often certain outcomes occur.

Rather than giving a single forecast, it gives you a range of possibilities, based on the distributions of your assumptions.

Example

Let's say your monthly revenue depends on three variables:

- **Volume** (with variability)
- **Price** (with a range)
- **Conversion rate** (with uncertainty)

Instead of assuming fixed values, you assume:

- Volume ~ Normal(10,000, 500)
- Price ~ Normal($50, $5)
- Conversion rate ~ Uniform(0.80, 0.90)

You run the model 5,000 times, each time drawing random values from these distributions. The result is a distribution of revenue outcomes, not just one.

Why Use Simulation in Finance?

Monte Carlo simulation helps answer questions like these:

- What's the probability that revenue will fall below $1M next quarter?
- How much cash do we need on hand to cover 95% of downside scenarios?
- Which product mix leads to the most stable margin?
- How sensitive is earnings before interest and taxes (EBIT) to input cost volatility?

In short: simulations help quantify uncertainty and risk in a way that static forecasts cannot.

Prompting AI to Build a Monte Carlo Simulation

Let's walk through a basic example.
Prompt:

> "Generate Python code to run a Monte Carlo simulation of monthly revenue over the next six months.
>
> Assume:
>
> - Volume is normally distributed with mean = 10,000 and std = 500.

- Price is normally distributed with mean = $50 and std = $5.
- Conversion rate is uniformly distributed between 0.80 and 0.90.

  Calculate revenue as Volume × Price × Conversion

  Run the simulation 10,000 times and plot the distribution of outcomes using a histogram."

  The AI will return the following:

- Imports for numpy, matplotlib, pandas
- A loop or vectorized calculation for 10,000 iterations
- A histogram of the simulated revenue distribution
- Summary statistics (mean, median, 5th/95th percentile)

You can then prompt:

"Add vertical lines for the 5th and 95th percentile to show the risk bounds."

Use Case: Cash Flow Simulation

Suppose your cash inflows and outflows vary month to month. You want to know how often you'll fall below a critical cash threshold.

Prompt:

"Simulate 12 months of cash flow with:

- Inflows normally distributed: mean = $800K, std = $100K
- Outflows normally distributed: mean = $750K, std = $90K

Start with $1.5M in cash.
Run 5,000 simulations and count how often ending cash falls below $500K."

The AI will generate the code, loop through each simulation, and return this:

- A histogram of final cash positions

- The percentage of simulations that fall below the threshold (your "risk probability")

You can use this to guide decisions on these issues:

- Capital raises
- Cost reduction targets
- Revenue floor planning

Use Case: Pricing Strategy Simulation

Imagine you're considering a price change but are unsure how it will affect demand.

Prompt:

"Simulate revenue under three pricing strategies: $45, $50, $55. For each price point, assume:

- Volume response is normally distributed, and inversely related to price
- Revenue = Volume × Price

Run 10,000 simulations per strategy
Plot the revenue distributions side by side and summarize the average and downside risk for each."

AI will generate the following:

- Three sets of simulations
- Side-by-side histograms or boxplots
- Summary statistics for comparison

This lets you see not only which strategy has the highest expected revenue but also which has the lowest volatility or risk of loss.

Using AI to Summarize Simulation Outputs

Once you've run your simulation, AI can help you interpret it for decision-making.

Prompt:

"Write a three-sentence summary of the simulation results:

- What's the average outcome?
- What's the range between 5th and 95th percentile?
- What recommendation would you make based on this?"

You'll get clear messaging that you can include in decks, emails, or leadership updates.

AI is especially helpful in these situations:

- You want multiple stakeholders to understand probabilistic risk.
- You need to write recommendations in business language.
- You're preparing slide notes or commentary on the outputs.

Creating Recommendation Engines Based on Simulations

Simulation outputs are great—but even better when they drive action.

You can prompt:

"Based on the simulation, if the probability of a shortfall exceeds 10%, recommend three actions to mitigate the risk."

Or:

"Suggest threshold triggers for CFO review based on the lower bound of the simulation range."

Now you're not just modeling outcomes—you're operationalizing insights.

Other examples:

- **Trigger reforecasting** if a revenue simulation falls below a certain bound
- **Adjust budget buffers** based on cash flow simulation volatility
- **Rebalance portfolio mix** if product simulations show concentrated risk

AI helps translate numbers into actions.

Summary Table: Monte Carlo Simulation Prompts

Goal	Sample Prompt
Model uncertainty in revenue	"Run Monte Carlo simulation of revenue using distributions for volume, price, and conversion."
Simulate cash runway	"Simulate 12 months of inflows/outflows and calculate ending cash under volatility."
Compare pricing strategies	"Simulate and compare revenue at different price points with demand variation."
Estimate risk probability	"What % of simulations fall below our EBIT target?"
Generate recommendations	"Summarize simulation results and suggest three mitigations for downside risk."

Monte Carlo simulation brings a new level of sophistication—and realism—to finance decision-making. It acknowledges what all experienced professionals know: the future is uncertain, and the best decisions are made not on averages, but on distributions.

With AI, the barrier to using simulation is gone. You don't need to know statistics, model logic, or how to code loops. You just need to describe the following:

- Your assumptions
- Your business drivers
- The question you want answered

AI takes care of the rest: writing the code, visualizing the output, summarizing the insights, and even suggesting actions.

Building Actionable Decision Frameworks with AI

You've seen how AI can help simulate risks, run optimizations, and model complex scenarios. But to truly drive value, those outputs need to lead to real-world decisions—presented in a way that is understandable, defensible, and aligned with business priorities.

This is where decision frameworks come into play. A decision framework brings structure to ambiguity. It helps finance professionals—and their stakeholders—move from "what the data says" to "what we should do, why, and with what trade-offs." With AI, building these frameworks becomes more efficient, more consistent, and more collaborative.

Why Decision Frameworks Matter in Finance

Finance teams sit at the intersection of strategy and execution. We're the ones who ask:

- Can we afford this?
- What will the impact be?
- What are the risks?
- What are the alternatives?

But without structure, financial advice can feel vague—or worse, biased.

That's where frameworks help. They force us to do the following:

- Lay out assumptions clearly.
- Weigh trade-offs openly.
- Show alternatives, not just one option.
- Highlight what we know and don't know.

- Align financial models with business priorities.

And they allow leadership to make informed, confident decisions.

Prompting AI to Build a Decision Matrix

A simple yet powerful decision tool is the decision matrix—a table that compares multiple options across defined criteria (impact, cost, risk, feasibility, etc.).

Prompt:

"Create a decision matrix comparing three cost reduction options:

- Freeze hiring
- Reduce contractor budget
- Cut marketing spend

Criteria: impact on cost, impact on operations, speed of implementation, risk
Score each on a 1–5 scale and add a final recommendation row."

AI will output a clean matrix like this:

Option	Cost Impact	Operational Risk	Speed	Overall Score
Freeze Hiring	4	2	5	11
Cut Contractor Budget	5	3	4	12
Cut Marketing Spend	3	4	3	10

You can then prompt:

"Summarize the trade-offs in a short paragraph for an executive audience."

Now you've gone from financial logic to decision-ready insight.

Building Structured Trade-Off Narratives

Decision frameworks aren't always numerical. Sometimes the goal is to show the logic behind a recommendation.

AI can help you write structured comparisons like this:

"Compare the trade-offs between investing $1M in a new product line vs expanding the sales team by 15 headcount. Include expected ROI, time to value, strategic alignment, and potential risks."

AI will return a paragraph for each option, followed by a conclusion.

You can refine with this:

"Make the tone executive-level and focus on strategic implications."

This helps you communicate *why* the recommendation matters—not just what it is.

Using AI to Draft Executive Recommendations

Once your model, simulation, or optimization is complete, you'll need to package the result into a clear recommendation. AI can help you do this fast.

Prompt:

"Based on the optimization model results, write a slide summary:

- Option selected
- Key drivers behind it
- Benefits
- Risks
- Assumptions used

Keep it concise and bullet-pointed."

This becomes a plug-and-play slide for your chief financial officer (CFO), vice president, or board deck.

You can also prompt:

"Write a script for presenting this recommendation in a steering committee."

The AI-generated script can help you do the following:

- Sequence your message clearly.
- Address anticipated objections.
- Sound prepared and confident.

Building Repeatable Frameworks for Finance Teams

As with prompting and forecasting, the goal is not just a one-time output. You want to create reusable structures that standardize how your team approaches decisions.

AI can help you do the following:

- Build templates for investment case evaluations.
- Create reusable prompt libraries for trade-off analysis.
- Develop checklists for risk-adjusted recommendations.
- Standardize how assumptions are documented.

Prompt:

"Create a checklist to evaluate a financial recommendation before presenting it to executives. Include items like are all assumptions documented, are alternatives shown, is risk assessed, is the impact quantified?"

You can then turn that into a shared team resource.

Auditable and Transparent Decision Support

One of the strengths of using AI + code-driven analysis is that your logic becomes more transparent. You can show the following:

- What assumptions were made
- What scenarios were run
- What constraints were applied
- What model or method was used

This improves these issues:

- Auditability
- Stakeholder trust
- Internal alignment

Prompt:

"Summarize the input assumptions and constraints used in this model in a format suitable for documentation or audit trails."

You can also ask:

"What questions might a CFO or board member ask about this recommendation? Help me prepare responses."

AI becomes not just a calculator—but a sounding board for preparation.

Telling the Story of the Decision

Finance professionals who succeed at the highest levels do more than model—they tell the story of the decision.
AI can help you build this narrative:

"Write a one-page briefing that walks through:

- The context for the decision
- The options considered

- The analysis performed
- The recommendation
- Key risks and next steps."

This becomes your talking memo, email summary, or pre-read for a decision meeting.

Best Practices for AI-Enabled Decision Frameworks

To close the loop, here are six best practices for building actionable decision frameworks with AI:

1. **Start with the question:** What decision are we supporting? What's at stake?
2. **Lay out the options:** Don't just present the winner. Show what was considered.
3. **Structure assumptions:** Keep them visible, editable, and reviewable.
4. **Present trade-offs:** Use matrices, side-by-side comparisons, or visuals.
5. **Tie back to business goals:** Show how the recommendation supports strategy, not just numbers.
6. **Document for scale:** Turn strong prompts into templates your team can reuse.

Final Thoughts

Prescriptive analytics doesn't end when the model is solved. It ends when a decision is made—and that decision leads to action. AI gives finance professionals the tools to not just analyze but to advise and influence.

You've now learned how to do the following:

- Use AI to build decision matrices and narratives.
- Turn simulation and optimization outputs into executive recommendations.

- Structure assumptions, alternatives, and risks transparently.
- Scale your approach with repeatable, auditable templates.
- Lead decisions with clarity, structure, and impact.

In Chapter 8, we'll move into automation—where AI not only helps you make better decisions but also begins to take repetitive work off your plate. You'll learn how to use Python, Power Query, and AI tools like n8n to automate financial workflows across planning, reporting, and analysis.

Chapter 8

Automation in FP&A—Doing More with Less

The Case for Automation in Finance

In many finance teams, automation still feels like a luxury—something reserved for information technology (IT) teams, data engineers, or large companies with dedicated digital transformation departments. But that mindset is quickly becoming outdated.

In today's AI-enabled world, automation is no longer optional for modern finance teams—it's essential.

Whether it's importing and cleaning data, refreshing reports, reconciling mismatched records, or generating monthly commentary, most of the work done in financial planning and analysis (FP&A) and controllership functions is repetitive, rules-based, and time-consuming. And it doesn't scale.

AI and lightweight coding tools like Python, Power Query, and no-code platforms now make it possible for finance professionals themselves to automate these workflows—without relying entirely on developers or external consultants.

This chapter is about giving you the tools, language, and mindset to do exactly that.

Manual Work Is the Hidden Bottleneck in Finance

The typical finance function is still powered by spreadsheets, shared folders, and hours of manual processing.

You might recognize some of these:

- Downloading reports from three different systems, combining them manually
- Cleaning inconsistent date formats, naming conventions, or missing values
- Copy-pasting financials into a PowerPoint deck for a monthly meeting
- Checking a long list of cost center variances by hand
- Sending the same reminder email to business partners every quarter

None of this work is strategic. None of it creates differentiated value. But it takes hours every week.

And it's not just about time. Manual work introduces the potential problems:

- **Risk of error:** A single misplaced decimal or link can undermine decision-making.
- **Lack of scalability:** Your processes break down when the data grows or the team changes.
- **Burnout:** Skilled professionals doing work that should be automated.

The opportunity is clear: eliminate or reduce manual processes and redirect time and energy toward analysis, insight, and impact.

What's Changed? AI Has Lowered the Barrier

In the past, automating financial workflows required technical skill. You needed to know multiple skills:

- How to write Python scripts
- How to schedule jobs on a server
- How to clean and structure data programmatically
- How to interact with APIs or databases

These are still useful skills, but they're no longer mandatory.

Thanks to large language models, you can now describe the task you want to automate—and the AI will write the logic.

Example:

"I receive a monthly Excel file with sales data in messy format. Generate a Python script that does the following:

- Loads the file
- Removes empty rows
- Fills missing dates
- Groups data by region and product
- Outputs a cleaned file for reporting"

The AI returns working Python code. You test it. You refine the prompt. And now you have a *reusable automation*—built by you, not handed off to someone else.

The friction is gone.

What Tasks Are Ready for Automation?

Not every task should be automated, but many of the most time-consuming ones are perfect candidates.

A good automation candidate in finance has at least three of the following:

- **Repeatable:** It happens weekly, monthly, or quarterly.
- **Rules-based:** The logic doesn't change much each time.
- **Time-consuming:** It takes longer than 15–20 minutes.
- **Manual steps:** You're moving files, reformatting, copying, pasting.
- **Error-prone:** Small mistakes can create big problems.
- **Scalable:** The same logic could apply to multiple entities, departments, or data sources.

Let's look at some common examples.

Month-End Reporting

- Importing multiple Excel or CSV files
- Aggregating numbers by cost center
- Comparing actuals versus budget
- Generating variance commentary
- Sending email notifications

Planning and Forecasting

- Updating base assumptions from source files
- Refreshing drivers (e.g., volume, pricing, headcount)
- Rolling forward forecasts
- Generating updated charts and slides

Ad Hoc Analysis

- Reconciling numbers between systems
- Performing the same calculations across different inputs
- Looking for outliers or rule violations
- Running the same dashboard refresh logic

These tasks don't require intelligence—they require structure. And AI can help you build that structure automatically.

Why Finance Professionals Are Uniquely Positioned to Automate

Here's the counterintuitive insight: *you don't need to be a developer to build automation.* In fact, the best automation often comes from those closest to the process.

As a finance professional, you can do the following:

- Know the business logic behind the numbers.
- Understand the constraints and exceptions.
- Know what "done right" looks like.
- Have the motivation to make the process better.

With AI, you now also have the following:

- A tool that can generate Python scripts from plain English
- A guide that can explain each line of logic if you're unsure
- A partner that lets you test and refine until it works

This combination—domain knowledge + AI—makes you more effective than a technical expert with no business context.

And most important: you don't need to write perfect code. You just need to describe the goal clearly.

A Simple Framework for Getting Started

If you're new to automation, start with a few simple steps:

1. **Identify a pain point:** Look for a task you do repeatedly that's time-consuming or tedious.
2. **Describe it clearly:** Break the task into steps in natural language.
3. **Prompt the AI:.** Use a clear, structured prompt that explains:
    - The input (e.g., Excel file, CSV, dataframe)
    - The action (e.g., clean, merge, calculate, summarize)
    - The output (e.g., new file, chart, email)

4. **Test the result:** Run the code in Google Colab or Excel (if it's Power Query or Python-in-Excel).
5. **Refine and save:** Make improvements, then save the prompt and script for reuse.
6. **Document the logic:** Add comments or ask AI to explain each part for your future self or team.

You'll learn quickly, and the returns will grow with every task you automate.

The Mindset Shift: From Analyst to Builder

The biggest change isn't technical—it's mental. Once you realize that you can build your own tools, design your own processes, and delegate work to AI, not just coworkers, you start operating differently.

You're no longer just completing tasks—you're *designing systems*.

And the time you reclaim? You can spend that on these actions instead:

- Driving strategic initiatives
- Exploring new models
- Communicating insights
- Leading transformation

This is the new skill set for finance leaders: analyst and automation architect.

Automation is not about removing people. It's about removing friction. It's about letting finance professionals focus on the work that actually moves the business forward.

You now have access to tools that were once reserved for developers. And with AI as your guide, you don't need to master the syntax—you need to master the logic of your own processes.

In the next sections of this chapter, we'll go deeper into these functions:

- Using Python to automate recurring FP&A tasks
- Leveraging Power Query and Copilot inside Excel and Power BI
- Using low-code platforms like n8n to chain together full workflows
- Building a repeatable automation practice inside your team

You don't have to automate everything at once. Just start with one task—and you'll never go back.

Using Python to Automate Everyday Finance Tasks

As I've mentioned, if there's one tool that bridges the gap between finance work and automation, it's Python.

It's not the only option—and we'll cover Power Query and low-code platforms next—but it's uniquely powerful because it offers so much:

- Complete control over data inputs and outputs
- Integration with every file format finance works with (CSV, Excel, PDF, SQL)
- A large set of open-source libraries built specifically for analysis and automation
- The ability to run scripts locally, in the cloud, or inside notebooks like Google Colab

And, thanks to AI, you no longer need to learn Python the way developers do. You just need to understand your process clearly, and know how to prompt AI to write the logic for you.

In this section, we'll look at the following:

- What kinds of finance tasks Python is great at automating
- How to prompt AI to generate automation scripts

- The most useful Python libraries for finance workflows
- How to run and reuse these scripts using Google Colab or your desktop
- Real examples of automating your daily, weekly, and monthly tasks

Why Python Is So Useful for Automation

Most finance workflows revolve around four things:

1. **Importing** data from different sources (Excel, CSV, SQL)
2. **Transforming** or cleaning it (dates, joins, formatting)
3. **Calculating** new outputs (ratios, summaries, flags)
4. **Exporting** the result (new file, chart, email, report)

Python is perfect for these because it can do the following:

- Handle files of any size or structure.
- Automate the same process across 10, 50, or 500 files.
- Replace repetitive Excel formulas with clean, readable logic.
- Integrate with email, APIs, file systems, and databases.

More important: *you don't have to write the code yourself.*
Just prompt AI with the task, and it will do the heavy lifting.

How to Prompt AI to Write Python Automation Code

Let's walk through a simple automation.

Use Case:

You receive a raw Excel file every month with revenue data. You need to do the following:

- Clean the headers.
- Remove blank rows.

- Group by Region and Product.
- Save a cleaned file for use in reporting.

Prompt:

"Generate a Python script using pandas that:

- Loads an Excel file called Revenue_Raw.xlsx
- Cleans up column names (strip spaces, lowercase)
- Removes empty rows
- Groups data by Region and Product and sums Revenue
- Saves the output to Revenue_Cleaned.xlsx"

AI will give you working code that does the following:

- Reads the file with pd.read_excel()
- Uses df.columns = df.columns.str.strip().str.lower()
- Drops empty rows with df.dropna()
- Groups with df.groupby(['region', 'product']).sum()
- Writes to Excel with df.to_excel()

You now have a reusable, testable script you can run every month in 30 seconds.

Automating Reporting Workflows

Here are some other common tasks you can automate with Python.

Combine Multiple Excel Files

"I have a folder with 12 Excel files, each for a different month. Generate Python code that:

- Loads all files
- Stacks the data together
- Filters for Region = 'Europe'
- Saves to one combined Excel file."

Create Monthly Commentary Automatically

"Using a dataframe with actuals versus budget by cost center, generate a text commentary that summarizes:

- Top three variances
- Cost centers over budget by more than 10%
- Total over/under budget amount"

AI will write logic that sorts, filters, and generates human-readable text for your reporting pack.

Automate Chart Creation

"Create a bar chart showing revenue by product for the last six months.
Save the chart as a PNG image."
Great for reports, dashboards, or presentations.

How to Run These Scripts Easily (Google Colab)

You don't need to install Python on your laptop or set up complex environments. Use Google Colab—a free, browser-based Python notebook provided by Google.

Steps:

1. Go to colab.research.google.com.
2. Click "New Notebook."
3. Paste your AI-generated code.
4. Upload your Excel files using the upload button.
5. Run the cells (Shift+Enter).

This is fast, free, and secure. You can even share the notebook like a Google Doc.

Once you're comfortable, you can do the following:

- Reuse the same script monthly.
- Turn it into a template for other files.
- Build out multiple steps into one workflow.

What to Include in a Good Prompt for Python Automation

To get clean, working code from AI, include these four elements in your prompt:

1. **Where the data is stored**
   - File name? Folder? Format? Sheet name?
2. **What action needs to be done**
   - Clean? Group? Merge? Filter?
3. **Any rules or logic**
   - Ignore missing rows? Sum by cost center? Rename columns?
4. **What the output should be**
   - New file? Chart? Email? Table?

Example:

"Generate Python code that loads all CSV files in a folder called Sales_2024/, filters for 'Product A,' groups by month, sums revenue, and outputs a line chart with labeled axes."

From Scripts to Automation: Scheduling with Python

Once your script is working, you can even schedule it to run automatically.
   Ask AI:

"Modify this script to run every Monday at 7 a.m. and send the resulting Excel file to my email using SMTP."

It will return the following:

- A schedule function that triggers weekly
- An smtplib email routine
- A full automation loop

While this may require basic setup on your machine or server, AI walks you through it step-by-step.

Documentation and Reusability

You can also ask AI to do this:

- Add comments to your code.
- Create a README explaining how to run it.
- Break your script into reusable functions.
- Convert it into a template you can reuse for different datasets.

Prompt:
"Comment each line of this script to explain what it does. Then write a short guide on how to run it in Google Colab."

You don't need to be a Python expert to automate your finance work. You just need this:

- Clear process logic
- A structured prompt
- A few iterations of testing and refining

Python + AI gives you the power to do the following:

- Save hours on repetitive tasks.
- Reduce risk of manual errors.
- Deliver faster, cleaner, more consistent outputs.

You're not replacing your job—you're replacing busywork with code that works for you.

In the next section, we'll turn to Power Query—an automation engine hidden inside Excel and Power BI. You'll learn how to use AI to generate M code, clean data, build queries, and transform files inside tools you already use every day.

Power Query + AI—Automating in Excel and Power BI

If Python is the most powerful general-purpose tool for finance automation, then Power Query is the most accessible and underused.

Why? Because it's already embedded in Excel and Power BI—the tools finance teams use daily—and it doesn't require any programming knowledge to get started.

Power Query lets you build repeatable data workflows inside your spreadsheet or business information (BI) dashboards:

- Automatically clean and format messy datasets.
- Merge multiple tables.
- Unpivot columns for better modeling.
- Apply logic like "if/then" conditions and calculated columns.
- Refresh data sources with a single click (or automatically).

With AI tools like ChatGPT, Copilot for Excel, and Power BI, you can now go one step further: use natural language prompts to generate, fix, and enhance Power Query logic.

This section will show you how to do the following:

- Use AI to write and troubleshoot Power Query formulas (M code).
- Automate repetitive Excel data prep.
- Build refreshable Power BI datasets.
- Design structured prompts to create robust transformation logic.
- Connect AI-assisted data wrangling to your broader automation workflow.

What Is Power Query (and Why Should You Use It)?

Power Query is a data transformation engine built into these programs:

- Excel (on the "Data" tab under "Get & Transform Data")
- Power BI (it's the first step when loading or shaping any data)

Think of it as Excel's ETL layer—a way to extract, transform, and load data without using VBA or writing Python.

It works like a visual recipe:

- Each transformation step is recorded (filter, rename, merge, etc.).
- The steps are applied every time the data refreshes.
- You never overwrite your original data.
- You can connect to files, folders, databases, APIs, and more.

Why Finance Teams Should Automate with Power Query

Most finance professionals spend significant time doing things like the following:

- Cleaning inconsistent column headers
- Deleting extra rows or columns
- Standardizing date formats or currencies
- Merging budget and actuals
- Transposing or unpivoting tables for modeling

Power Query can do all of this—and repeat it instantly across new files or periods.

Common use cases:

- Automatically clean and import every month's transactional report.
- Merge cost center actuals with forecast from two Excel sources.

- Format headcount files for consistent payroll allocation.
- Refresh Power BI dashboards daily without manual prep.

Using AI to Write or Fix M Code

Power Query uses a scripting language called M behind the scenes. Most users don't write it manually—but with AI, you now can.

And, more important, you can ask AI to generate or troubleshoot it for you.

Example Prompt:

"Generate Power Query M code that:

- Loads a CSV file
- Filters rows where Region = 'EMEA'
- Renames columns to remove spaces
- Adds a new column that calculates Revenue per Unit = Revenue/Units
- Sorts by date descending"

The AI will generate valid M code you can paste into the "Advanced Editor" in Power Query.

This is extremely powerful in these situations:

- You want to apply a transformation not available in the graphical user interface.
- You have broken queries that throw errors.
- You want to replicate steps across files or tables.

How to Ask AI to Debug Power Query Errors

Let's say you get an error in your query: "Expression.Error: We cannot convert the value null to type Text."

You can copy the code and prompt:

"This Power Query M code throws an error: [paste code]. Explain what the error means and how to fix it."

The AI will identify which line is causing the issue and explain how to handle nulls or convert types appropriately.

Then you can ask:

"Update the code to handle null values in the CustomerName column by replacing them with 'Unknown.'"

This replaces long hours of googling with a conversational solution.

Automating Excel Data Prep with Power Query + AI

Here's a step-by-step automation flow for Excel data prep:

Use Case:
Each month, your team downloads a file called Sales_July2026.xlsx. It needs to be cleaned, filtered, and formatted before being loaded into your model.

Steps:

1. **Open Power Query Editor** in Excel.
2. Click "Get Data" → "From File" → "From Workbook."
3. Import your sheet.
4. Describe your cleaning steps in a prompt:
   "Write M code to:
   - Remove top two rows
   - Promote first row to headers
   - Remove columns 'Notes' and 'Status'
   - Change Date column to proper date format
   - Filter rows where Sales > 0"

5. Paste the M code into the Advanced Editor.
6. Save the query and connect it to your model tab.
7. Next month, just point the query to Sales_August2024.xlsx and hit Refresh.

No rework. No reformatting. Just click and go.

Power BI: Scaling the Same Logic to Dashboards

Everything you can do in Power Query for Excel, you can do at scale in Power BI.

Power BI relies on Power Query as the first layer of its modeling process. Every time you "Get Data," you are entering a Power Query environment.

In large datasets, AI + Power Query lets you do the following:

- Clean and combine hundreds of files from SharePoint or a folder.
- Automate data model prep across multiple departments.
- Create parameterized queries that adjust based on input.
- Handle currency conversions, calendar tables, and lookup merges dynamically.

Prompt example:

"I have a folder in SharePoint with monthly actuals by cost center.

Generate Power Query M code that:

- Loads all Excel files
- Filters to only the last three months
- Combines sheets with a standard layout
- Groups by Department and sums TotalCost
- Loads into Power BI for dashboarding"

Best Practices for Prompting AI in Power Query Workflows

To get high-quality output from AI for Excel and Power BI automation, include the following:

1. **Where the data is**
   - File type, folder, source system
2. **What transformations you need**
   - Cleaning steps, filters, joins, calculated columns
3. **The structure of the data**
   - Column names, expected formats
4. **The output format or behavior**
   - New table, loaded to model, formatted for reporting

Example:

"I have two Excel files: Budget2026.xlsx and Actuals2026.xlsx. Each has a sheet named 'P&L.'
I want M code to:

- Load both files
- Merge on AccountCode and CostCenter
- Create a column for variance = Actual—Budget
- Filter for variances > 10%
- Load to Excel sheet called 'VarianceReport'"

Low-Code and No-Code Automation Tools: n8n, Zapier, Make

Even if you've never written a line of code—or don't want to—you can still automate finance workflows.

That's the promise of the low-code and no-code movement, and platforms like n8n, Zapier, and Make (formerly Integromat) are leading the way.

These tools are designed for people who understand processes but may not have technical experience. Instead of writing scripts, you build automations using drag-and-drop blocks or visual flowcharts.

And now with AI as a partner, you don't even need to know *how* to build the flow—you just need to describe what you want to automate. The AI can help you accomplish the following:

- Design the logic.
- Choose the right tools.
- Build the steps.
- Troubleshoot errors.

For finance teams, this is a huge unlock.

What Are Low-Code Automation Tools?

These tools connect different apps and services using a visual workflow builder. You can set up *triggers* (when something happens) and *actions* (what should happen next).

For example:

- **Trigger:** A new Excel file is added to a SharePoint folder.
- **Action:** Clean the data using Python.
- **Action:** Email the report to your team.
- **Action:** Post a summary in Slack.

Each of these steps is added as a visual block. You don't write any code—you just define the logic.

Popular platforms:

- **n8n:** Open-source, customizable, advanced (recommended for finance teams with IT support)
- **Zapier:** Extremely user-friendly, broad app integration, limited logic control
- **Make:** Visual and powerful, good for complex multistep workflows

Why These Tools Matter for Finance

Most finance work today happens across multiple systems:

- Excel/Google Sheets
- SharePoint/Google Drive
- ERP systems (SAP, Oracle, NetSuite)
- Power BI/Tableau
- Email/Slack
- Payroll, CRM, HRIS

Manually connecting these systems is slow, error-prone, and expensive.

But now, with tools like n8n or Zapier, you can do the following:

- Automate data handoffs (e.g., from system exports to dashboards).
- Trigger alerts when thresholds are breached.
- Move files when workflows complete.
- Post updates in Slack or Teams automatically.
- Schedule recurring reports without touching them.

And best of all: AI can now help you build these workflows.

How to Prompt AI to Build Low-Code Automation Workflows

Even though these platforms are visual, it's useful to *describe* your desired workflow in a structured prompt. That way, AI can help you build it before you even open the tool.

Example Prompt:

"I want to automate our weekly cash report process:

- Trigger: A new Excel file is added to a folder called Cash_Forecasts
- Step 1: Clean the file using a Python script in Google Colab

- Step 2: Save the cleaned file to another folder called ReadyToSend
- Step 3: Email the cleaned file to the CFO and Finance Director
- Step 4: Post a message in our Slack channel #cash-updates"

You can then ask:

"Which tool should I use (Zapier, n8n, or Make), and how would the flow look step-by-step?"

AI will return the following:

- The ideal platform (e.g., n8n for flexibility)
- A visual description of the nodes
- Which integrations to use (Google Drive, Gmail, Python webhook, Slack)
- Optional logic (e.g., only send if the report passes validation)

Common Finance Workflows to Automate

Here are a few finance-specific use cases that are a great fit for low-code/no-code platforms:

- **Automated Report Distribution**
  1. **Trigger:** New file is added to SharePoint.
  2. **Action:** Rename, zip, and email the file.
  3. **Action:** Log the delivery in a tracking sheet.

- **Slack Alerts for Thresholds**
  1. **Trigger:** A KPI file is updated in Google Sheets.
  2. **Action:** If Gross Margin < 30%, send Slack alert to #finance-alerts.

- **Dashboard Refresh Notification**
  1. **Trigger:** Power BI dataset refresh completes.
  2. **Action:** Post message with link to updated dashboard.

- **Expense Approval Flow**
  1. **Trigger:** New row added in "Pending Expenses" spreadsheet.
  2. **Action:** Send summary via email to manager.
  3. **Action:** If approved, move row to "Approved Expenses."

- **Quarter-End Checklist Automation**
  1. **Trigger:** First day of Q4.
  2. **Action:** Create checklist tasks in project management tool.
  3. **Action:** Notify relevant owners with deadlines.

These workflows often fall between finance and operations—so owning them builds cross-functional value.

How to Connect Python or Excel into No-Code Flows

Many teams ask, "Can I connect my Python script into these platforms?" The answer is yes.

Most platforms allow you to do the following:

- Call a webhook that triggers a script (hosted on Google Colab, AWS Lambda, or other).
- Run a Python function directly (in tools like n8n).
- Use services like Zapier Webhooks, or Make HTTP modules to integrate APIs.

Prompt example:
"I want to trigger a Google Colab script that runs a reconciliation model when a new file is uploaded to a folder. The script should run, return a status message, and send an email if there are mismatches."

AI will return a logic diagram and recommendations on how to do the following:

- Host your Python function.
- Trigger it via webhook.

- Pass parameters (like the file name or path).
- Handle the response.

This bridges the gap between code-based power and no-code orchestration.

Best Practices for Building Reliable Workflows

Here I offer some of the best practices to create workflows:

1. **Start small:** Begin with a single, low-risk workflow (like file naming or notifications).
2. **Describe steps clearly before building:** Use structured prompts to get AI's help planning.
3. **Use error handling:** Add fallback steps (e.g., send alert if a file isn't found or fails to process).
4. **Document your workflows:** AI can help generate a process doc or flowchart to share with your team.
5. **Test with real data:** Don't wait until quarter-end—test in live conditions.
6. **Use logs:** Track which runs succeed, fail, or are skipped.

Low-code and no-code automation tools allow finance professionals to become workflow designers, not just data handlers. When paired with AI, these tools enable you to build systems that do the following:

- Move data across platforms.
- Trigger models or alerts.
- Communicate automatically with your team.
- Save hours every month—without writing code.

Building a Sustainable Automation Culture in Finance

By this point, you've seen that AI makes it possible for anyone in finance—whether an analyst, controller, or chief financial officer—to build automations. You've learned how to use Python,

Power Query, and low-code tools like n8n to eliminate repetitive work and build more resilient processes.

But automation isn't just about tools. To truly transform how your team operates, you need something more enduring: a culture of automation.

That means shifting from one-off improvements to a systematic way of working. It means turning every manual process into an opportunity to save time, reduce risk, and elevate your team's strategic impact.

Automation Is a Mindset, Not Just a Tool

You don't build a culture by automating one report. You build it by changing how people think about work.

That starts with a simple shift in how you and your team respond to everyday tasks.

- Instead of asking, "How do I do this?"
  Ask, "How could I automate this?"
- Instead of saying, "I'll do it again next week,"
  Ask, "Can this be made repeatable?"
- Instead of rebuilding from scratch,
  Ask, "Is there a prompt or script I've used before?"

This mindset opens the door to scalable, reusable, teachable workflows.

Automation becomes not just a technical project, but part of your team's operating system.

Create a Personal and Team Prompt Library

You've learned how to write prompts for Python, Power Query, forecasting, decision support, and automation. But without structure, these valuable prompts get lost in Notion pages, Google Docs, or old chat windows.

That's why you need a prompt library.
Start with your own. Then expand to a shared team version.
How to structure it:

- **By function:** Reporting, Planning, Forecasting, Commentary, Dashboards, Reconciliations
- **By tool:** ChatGPT, Copilot, Python, Power BI, Power Query, n8n
- **By use case:** "Summarize actuals versus forecast," "Clean Excel columns," "Generate variance commentary," and so on
- **By file:** Link to saved code, scripts, or notebooks when available

You can even prompt AI to help you:
"Create a markdown template for organizing a prompt library by use case, including prompt text, example inputs, output type, and tool used."

This gives your team a single source of truth for automation—something that grows with every new use case.

Organize Automations by Finance Function

As your team builds more automations, they'll fall into natural categories.

Here's a simple framework for organizing them:

Function	Common Automations
FP&A	Forecast roll forwards, assumption updates, variance alerts
Controllership	Reconciliations, journal entry validation, closing checklists
Reporting	Data imports, dashboard refreshes, commentary generation
Treasury	Cash position reports, foreign exchange exposure monitoring
Tax	Data pulls for filings, threshold-based alerts

Use this categorization to do the following:

- Assign automation ownership by team or process.
- Audit and review workflows regularly.
- Spot opportunities to build shared tools or reusable components.

Build Prompt Templates into Your Team's Toolkit

Once a prompt works, template it. Think of it like a standardized formula or reusable block of logic.

Instead of starting from scratch each time, a team member can open a template that says:

"To generate monthly commentary, use this prompt structure:

- Context: 'I have a dataframe with actuals vs budget'
- Timeframe: 'for July 2026'
- Logic: 'identify top three variances, and write plain-English summary'"

Templates reduce cognitive load. They make automation scalable, consistent, and trainable.

Store them in these places:

- Your team's knowledge base (Notion, Confluence, SharePoint)
- Your prompt library
- AI tools that allow custom instructions (e.g., custom GPTs, AI copilots)

Educate and Enable Your Team

One person automating everything doesn't scale. You need distributed automation capacity—where each person knows how to spot opportunities and get started.

How to build this:

- **Start with a show-and-tell culture:** At weekly meetings, ask. "Who saved time with automation this week?"
- **Run internal training:** Teach your team how to write prompts, build with AI, and use basic Python or Power Query. Use short, live demos.
- **Create internal champions:** Find the analysts or managers most excited about this, and support them in experimenting.
- **Document learnings:** Every new automation should come with notes: what it does, how it works, when to use it.

Watch for Risks and Add Guardrails

Automation creates speed—but also introduces risk if unmanaged. Common pitfalls:

- Overreliance on a single person who built a process
- Poor documentation of logic
- Unvalidated assumptions or thresholds
- Shadow processes running without oversight

Mitigate these with:

- Code reviews or prompt reviews before production use
- Version control (even basic folders or naming conventions help)
- Access controls—who can run or edit scripts?
- Fallbacks and alerts—what happens when the automation fails?

This is one example prompt for an AI tool to help you design these checks:

"Create a checklist for reviewing a finance automation script before deployment."

Automation shouldn't mean losing control. It should mean fewer surprises, more reliability.

Embed Automation into Key Workflows

The best automations aren't side projects. They're part of how the team runs.

Opportunities to integrate automation include the following:

- **Month-end close:** Auto-reconcile, generate commentary, update checklists.
- **Budget cycles:** Roll forward models, refresh assumptions, send update prompts.
- **Quarterly reports:** Auto-pull KPIs, run narrative summaries, post drafts.
- **Board materials:** Generate charts, summaries, scenario comparisons.
- **Daily ops:** Trigger alerts, update dashboards, log activities.

For each recurring process, ask these questions:

- Where is the manual work?
- What decisions rely on it?
- What part could be triggered or refreshed automatically?

Then use AI to map and build the solution.

Final Thoughts

An automation culture doesn't mean every finance professional becomes a coder. It means this:

- Everyone knows how to identify repetitive work.
- Anyone can write a prompt to describe what should happen.
- The team has a shared library of solutions and scripts.
- Processes are documented, owned, and continuously improved.

In the same way Excel became a core skill in finance since the new millennium, AI-powered automation is the next evolution. It's not a bonus skill—it's a new baseline.

Congratulations, you now have the tools to do the following:

- Build automations with Python, Power Query, and low-code platforms.
- Use AI as your engineering partner.
- Create shared assets that save hours every week.
- Turn your finance team into a high-leverage, high-impact operation.

In Chapter 9, we'll look ahead to what's coming: emerging tools, AI agents, and the future of AI-native finance teams. You'll see how to prepare for change, evaluate new technologies, and lead your team into the next wave of transformation.

Chapter 9

Building Your AI Finance Stack

A Rapidly Changing Landscape—How AI Evolves Month by Month

If you feel like the world of artificial intelligence (AI) changes faster than you can keep up, that's because it does.

Since the public release of ChatGPT in late 2022, we've seen a pace of technological progress that's unprecedented. New models, tools, plugins, and platforms appear every month—each promising faster performance, better reasoning, cheaper access, or easier integration.

The truth is, AI is not a mature, static technology—it's a rapidly evolving ecosystem and that has big implications for finance professionals.

You may master a tool one month, only to find a better version the next. You may build an automation on one platform, and then a newer, simpler tool makes it obsolete. What was cutting-edge six months ago is now table stakes. What didn't exist a year ago may now be powering your team's daily workflow.

The key isn't to chase every new update. It's to develop a framework for evaluating AI tools and models over time. That way, you don't need to start from scratch every time something new appears—you can analyze, compare, and decide with confidence.

The AI Landscape Changes Every Month—Literally

In most areas of finance, tools and technologies evolve slowly. Excel has been around for decades. ERP systems update yearly. Budgeting software might change every five years.

AI isn't like that.

Since November 2022, we've seen these new products:

- GPT-3.5, GPT-4, and GPT-5
- Claude 1, 2, and 3 (Anthropic)
- Gemini (Google), from Bard to Gemini Pro to Gemini 2.5
- LLaMA 2 and 3 (Meta)
- Mistral and Mixtral models
- Falcon, Command-R, Zephyr, and dozens more open-source entrants

And this list only covers the large language models (LLMs)—not the apps, wrappers, copilots, or agent tools built on top of them.

Each release brings these advances:

- Better accuracy and reasoning
- Lower latency
- More context length (token capacity)
- Cheaper use
- More native integration with tools like Excel, Power BI, Slack, or Teams

It's a race. But you don't have to run after every new player. What you do need is a way to think clearly amidst the noise.

Why I'm Not Comparing All the Tools Here

You might expect this section to include a side-by-side comparison of all the major LLMs. But that would be outdated by the time you finish reading the book.

Instead, I'll give you something more valuable: a framework for evaluating any new AI tool or model, no matter when it launches or who builds it.

This framework is what I use when I evaluate a new model, platform, or AI assistant—and it's designed specifically with finance use cases in mind.

A Framework for Evaluating LLMs for Finance

When a new tool or model comes out, here's what I focus on:

- **Reasoning Quality**
  - Can it follow multistep financial logic?
  - Can it handle trade-offs, uncertainty, and ambiguity?
  - Does it reason through assumptions like a senior analyst would?
  - Can it explain its answer clearly in business terms?

  Most tools will summarize text and write emails. But for financial planning and analysis, forecasting, and planning, you need models that reason, not just generate.

- **Numerical Accuracy**
  - How well does it handle math?
  - Can it perform calculations without hallucinating?
  - Can it analyze tables, formulas, and structured data?

  Some models perform well on text but break down on numbers. If you're using AI for variance analysis or modeling logic, accuracy matters more than eloquence.

- **Context Window (Token Limit)**
  - How much information can the model handle in a single session?
  - Can you paste large Excel tables, datasets, or narratives into one prompt?
  - Can it remember earlier context across long conversations?

  Larger context windows (e.g., 128K tokens or more) enable you to work with more complex data, financial reports, or multisheet logic flows.

- **Speed and Cost**
  - How fast is the model's response?
  - Is it available in free tools or behind a paywall?
  - Can it be used at scale (e.g., across your team or department)?
  - Can it be embedded into your existing stack?

  Fast, affordable tools mean more adoption. If a model is 10× better but 100× more expensive, it may not be the right fit for your workflow.

- **Tool Integration**
  - Can it connect to Excel, Power BI, email, or databases?
  - Is there a plugin, API, or native integration?
  - Does it work inside Microsoft 365 Copilot, Google Sheets, or Slack?

  Finance professionals work in specific ecosystems. The best AI tool is the one that *fits into the tools you already use.*

- **Security and Governance**
  - Does the tool offer enterprise controls?
  - Can it be used safely with sensitive financial data?
  - Does it store prompts or data externally?

  Security is especially important in finance. You need confidence that what you paste into a prompt won't be used to train someone else's model.

You Don't Need to Try Everything—Just One or Two Tools That Fit You

The best advice I can give is this: pick one or two tools that work well for you—and get really good at using them.

You don't need to master every new model. You don't need to test every app. What you need is the following:

- A strong prompting habit
- A reliable tool for reasoning and generating code
- A working automation system (Python, Power Query, or no-code platform)
- A plan to improve your skills steadily over time

You'll get further by going deep than by skimming across every new launch.

How to Stay Informed Without Getting Overwhelmed

Here's a simple approach I follow:

1. **Choose a primary model to use day-to-day:** (e.g., ChatGPT, Microsoft Copilot, or Gemini).
2. **Every one to two months, evaluate what's changed:** Use trusted newsletters, podcasts, or AI update feeds from your favorite LinkedIn voice around AI for Finance—I try to post two or three times per week about these updates for example.
3. **Try a new tool only when it solves a new problem:** Don't switch models just because a new one claims to be better. Switch when it meets a specific need: better math, longer context, faster API, stronger integration.
4. **Document your findings in your own prompt library:** Keep notes on what worked, what didn't, and how the model responded.

This lets you stay curious—but grounded.

The AI landscape is changing too fast to memorize. So don't try to memorize it. Learn how to navigate it.

You've now got a framework for evaluating any AI tool, model, or platform:

- Reasoning quality
- Math accuracy
- Token context
- Speed and cost
- Integration fit
- Security posture

You don't need to know what comes next—you just need to know how to evaluate it when it does.

AI Agents, Autonomous Tools, and Self-Driving Finance

Most AI tools today work like assistants. You ask a question, and they give you an answer. You describe a process, and they write some code. It's a one-to-one interaction: prompt, respond, repeat.

But that model is beginning to evolve.

We're now entering the next phase: AI agents—systems that don't just respond, but act. They don't just answer a question, they pursue a goal. They can remember context across tasks, make decisions based on new information, and execute multistep workflows without constant user input.

This is the beginning of autonomous finance tooling. And while it's still early, the implications are huge.

Imagine a world where the following can happen:

- Your forecast refreshes itself daily, adjusting for actuals and new assumptions.
- Variance drivers are identified, explained, and summarized without your involvement.

- A new dataset lands in your SharePoint folder, and a system imports it, cleans it, runs diagnostics, updates dashboards, and pings the chief financial officer (CFO) in Slack.

This is self-driving finance—not in the sense of replacing you, but in automating the workflows you used to manage manually.

What Is an AI Agent?

An AI agent is a system that can do the following:

- Interpret a goal.
- Break it down into smaller tasks.
- Choose actions or tools to complete those tasks.
- Track progress.
- Adjust based on feedback.

In other words, it behaves more like a project manager than a search engine.

Unlike a chatbot, which responds to one prompt at a time, an agent can do the following:

- Run a loop of prompts, adjusting its own instructions.
- Use tools (APIs, databases, calculators) to gather or manipulate data.
- Decide when to stop, when to ask you for input, or when to escalate.

Agents combine multiple AI functions:

- Language understanding
- Planning and reasoning
- Memory or working context
- Action execution (via tools or plugins)

They can run in environments like the following:

- Local machines (AutoGPT, LangGraph)
- Cloud-based orchestrators (CrewAI, OpenAgents, Cognosys)
- Workflow tools with agent capabilities (n8n + AI plugins)

Use Cases for AI Agents in Finance

While the idea of an AI agent might sound abstract, it's already starting to impact core finance workflows.

Let's walk through a few examples that are emerging today.

1. **Rolling forecast agent:** You give the agent access to your data folder (actuals, assumptions, prior forecasts). Every day or week, it does the following:

   - Checks for new actuals
   - Runs the forecast update logic
   - Compares current forecast versus previous
   - Summarizes key changes
   - Sends output to a dashboard or email

   The goal isn't one-time analysis. It's ongoing, autonomous forecasting.

2. **Variance investigation agent:** Connect this to your enterprise resource planning (ERP) data or Power BI model. When actuals deviate from plan beyond a certain threshold, it can do the following:

   - Flags the variance.
   - Analyzes likely drivers.
   - Writes a short commentary with charts.
   - Suggests possible follow-up actions.

   It becomes your virtual analyst—running constantly, not just once a month.

3. **Data processing agent:** When a new file is uploaded, the agent can do the following:

   - Read and validate it.
   - Clean and transform the data.
   - Run reconciliation checks.
   - Log any issues.
   - Save clean output for the next workflow step.

   This reduces manual monitoring and makes processes reactive, not scheduled.

4. **Self-healing automation agent:** When one of your automations fails (e.g., a script error, bad input data), the agent can do the following:

   - Read the error.
   - Diagnose the likely cause.
   - Try a fix (e.g., change data types, re-run query).
   - Notify you only if it can't resolve the issue.

   It's not perfect—but it gives you a first line of support before a human needs to intervene.

How to Start Experimenting Safely

While agent technology is still early, you don't need to wait years to explore it. Here's how to start testing safely, even as a nontechnical finance professional.

1. **Use existing platforms that offer agent capabilities:** Some tools are starting to integrate agent-like features natively:

   - **OpenAI GPTs** with tools and memory
   - **CrewAI** for defining agent roles and toolchains
   - **LangChain** or **LangGraph** for more technical orchestration
   - **Zapier AI Actions** or **n8n AI plugins** for step-wise automation

You don't need to build your own AI agent from scratch. Start with a tool where agents are preconfigured and give it clear, sandboxed tasks.

2. **Start with a narrow, reversible process:** Don't start with critical month-end automation. Begin with the following:

   - Automating the refresh of a dashboard
   - Running daily summary emails of key performance indicators (KPIs)
   - Pulling data from a public API (e.g., fixed exchange rates, economic indicators)

   Limit what the agent can access. Don't give it database write access or ability to send emails without review.

3. **Pair agents with prompts, not just data:** Agents don't know what to do unless you tell them. Create a clear goal, context, and allowed actions.

   Example:

   "Every Monday, check if new actuals are available. If they are:

   - Run the forecast update script
   - Compare new vs previous forecast
   - Generate a short email summary draft
   - Save it to the 'Review' folder"

   Keep the loop tight. Agents work best when their goals are clearly defined and bounded.

Risks and Limitations of Agents Today

It's important to stay clear-eyed. While the vision of autonomous finance is exciting, AI agents still have limitations.

1. **Hallucination at scale:** An agent that loops incorrectly or makes wrong assumptions can cause damage faster than a manual tool.

   Mitigation:
   - Always test in sandbox mode.
   - Require review before actions are taken (e.g., send a draft, not a live email).

2. **Oversight and explainability:** It's not always clear why an agent made a decision. This is especially risky in finance where compliance, audit, and data lineage matter.

   Mitigation:
   - Log all steps and decisions.
   - Ask the agent to generate an "explanation" for each action.
   - Store logs for later review.

3. **Security and permissions:** Agents that can access file systems, APIs, or communication tools can potentially leak or misuse information.

   Mitigation:
   - Limit access.
   - Use read-only modes when possible.
   - Restrict runtime environments.

4. **Reliability and maintenance:** Agents aren't set and forget. They require monitoring, testing, and updates—just like any system.

   Mitigation:
   - Assign ownership.
   - Schedule regular reviews.
   - Treat them like software—not magic.

AI agents represent a major shift: from reactive prompts to proactive workflows. From tools you use occasionally, to systems that run alongside you continuously.

But the real value of agents isn't in replacing people—it's in amplifying what your team can do:

- Less time spent monitoring files
- Faster reactions to changing data
- Automated follow-ups and reporting
- Systems that keep running, even when you're not

Building AI-Native Finance Teams and Capabilities

AI is no longer just a tool that finance professionals can use—it's becoming a capability that finance teams must build.

The difference is subtle but significant.

Using AI means incorporating a model like ChatGPT or Copilot into a workflow. It might be a useful shortcut or productivity boost. But being AI-native means the function itself is structured on the reality that AI is part of the operating system.

It changes how you do these functions:

- Analyze and report
- Communicate and collaborate
- Hire, train, and evaluate
- Structure workflows and responsibilities

What Does It Mean to Be AI-Native?

For me, AI-native finance team doesn't just bolt AI onto legacy workflows. It builds new workflows on AI capabilities.

Here's how that looks in practice:

Area	Traditional Approach	AI-Native Approach
Forecasting	Analysts run updates monthly.	AI updates daily, humans interpret and adjust.
Reporting	Manual commentary is written after close.	Drafts are auto-generated, edited by team.
Variance Analysis	Ad hoc deep dives on exceptions.	AI flags variances and suggests drivers proactively.
Data Prep	Repeated Excel transformations	Automated pipelines with AI-augmented cleanup
Communication	Email and meetings to align	AI-generated summaries and recommendations for faster syncs

The biggest shift is not technical—it's cultural. Teams that become AI-native see themselves not just as operators, but as designers of systems. They stop asking, "What's the task today?" and start asking, "How should this work in a world where AI is part of the process?"

New Capabilities Your Team Will Need

As AI becomes more embedded in finance, the skills that matter most will shift. You don't need every team member to become a data scientist—but you do need to raise the baseline technical fluency across the board.

Here are the foundational capabilities of an AI-native finance team:

1. **Prompting with clarity and structure:** Everyone should know how to do the following:

   - Describe business problems clearly.
   - Write structured prompts that guide AI tools.
   - Iterate on prompts to improve accuracy.
   - Explain what they want and how the output will be used.

   Prompting is the new spreadsheet formula. It's not magic—it's literacy.

2. **Interpreting AI outputs critically:** Finance professionals will need to do the following:

   - Assess whether an AI-generated insight makes sense.
   - Spot when outputs are wrong or incomplete.
   - Ask follow-up questions or adjust assumptions.
   - Explain model outputs in business terms.

   You don't want blind acceptance. You want AI-assisted thinking, not AI outsourcing.

3. **Testing, debugging, and refining:** Every automation or analysis will need iteration. Analysts must be comfortable doing the following:

   - Testing scripts and prompts
   - Debugging errors (with AI's help)
   - Documenting logic and assumptions

   It's not about coding—it's about comfort with problem-solving using digital tools.

4. **Understanding data foundations:** You don't need every analyst writing SQL—but every finance professional should understand the following:

- What a dataset includes and doesn't
- How joins work
- What clean versus dirty data looks like
- How metrics are defined

This enables more informed collaboration with data, information technology, and AI tools.

Embedding AI in Hiring and Onboarding

As the finance function modernizes, so should your hiring.

Interview for Problem-Solvers, Not Just Technicians

The best AI-native finance professionals aren't the ones who know the most about tools—they're the ones who can think clearly about workflows.

Ask candidates how they would do the following:

- Automate a manual close process.
- Build a scalable forecast.
- Structure a dashboarding workflow.
- Train a junior analyst to use AI responsibly.

You're hiring designers, not just executors.

Onboard with Automation from Day One

Treat prompting, automation, and AI tools as part of your onboarding curriculum.

Give new team members these tools:

- A prompt library
- Example notebooks or workflows
- A short internal guide on "how we use AI in finance here"
- A sandbox environment to experiment safely

Normalize AI literacy from the start.

Cross-Functional Partnerships Will Matter More

As finance teams adopt AI, their interactions with other departments will change.

You'll need stronger partnerships with these areas:

- **Data and engineering:** For maintaining clean, accessible datasets
- **IT and security:** For compliant tool use, infrastructure, and risk management
- **Operations:** To design and execute processes with AI at the core
- **Product and strategy:** To align on metrics, goals, and decision frameworks

Finance won't just deliver reports—it will orchestrate systems. And that requires collaboration.

Build Feedback Loops into Workflows

AI-native teams build systems that learn and improve over time. That means:

- Capturing prompt performance (what worked, what didn't)
- Logging model errors or surprises
- Documenting human edits to AI-generated outputs
- Reviewing automations regularly for drift or exceptions

Use prompts like this:

"Summarize the last 10 runs of our forecast script. What changes occurred in assumptions? What outputs were overridden?"

Or:

"Suggest improvements to this prompt based on the last three outputs and their accuracy."

AI can help refine itself—but only if you create the loop.

Traits of High-Functioning AI-Native Teams

From what I've seen in my work with hundreds of finance professionals, the most successful AI-native teams share a few key traits:

Trait	Description
Tool-agnostic	They focus on workflows, not which tool is trendy this month.
Modular	They build workflows in pieces that can be improved or swapped.
Transparent	Their logic, assumptions, and scripts are open and documented.
Curious	They test new capabilities without chasing every shiny object.
Collaborative	They cocreate with data, IT, and ops—not just work in silos.
Iterative	They expect improvement to come from cycles of testing and feedback.

You don't need to be perfect. But you do need to start operating like a team that builds systems, not just maintains spreadsheets.

Becoming AI-native doesn't happen overnight. It's not about rolling out a new tool—it's about reshaping how your team thinks, operates, and creates value.

You don't have to wait for permission. Start with this:

- One well-documented automation
- One repeatable prompt library
- One clear standard for how AI is used in reports or forecasts

As more of your workflows run on AI, you'll naturally evolve from tool users to capability builders.

Leading the Transformation—Your Role in Shaping What Comes Next

In every era of transformation, some people wait to be told what to do—and others step up to shape what happens.

The finance profession is at one of those moments.

AI will reshape how we plan, analyze, forecast, report, and communicate. The question isn't whether it will happen. It's whether you want to be one of the people shaping how it happens.

And the good news is: you don't have to be a CFO, a developer, or a futurist to lead this change. You can lead from wherever you are—by building, sharing, improving, and inviting others along the way.

You Don't Need to Predict the Future—You Need to Build for It

People often ask, "Where is AI in finance going?"

Here's the truth: no one knows exactly. The tools, models, and interfaces are evolving too fast for anyone to map perfectly.

But you don't need a perfect map. You need a compass.

You don't need to predict which tool will dominate. You need to design systems that have the following qualities:

- Modular
- Documented
- Promptable
- Interpretable
- Reusable

That's how you future proof your work. Not by locking into one system—but by getting good at describing what good work looks like, regardless of the tool.

Build for flexibility, not finality.

From Tool User to System Designer

When AI first enters a team, most people use it like a search engine or assistant. They ask for code, get help with summaries, use it to explain or rewrite text.

That's fine. But it's not leadership.

Leading with AI means thinking like a system designer:

- "How should this process work now that AI exists?"
- "What steps can we automate? What decisions still need a human?"
- "How do we make this process repeatable, transparent, and improvable?"
- "What prompts or scripts should we build into the toolkit?"

You're not just using the tool—you're reshaping the workflow. You're asking better questions.

How to Lead AI Transformation from Any Level

1. **If you're an analyst:** You may not own the road map—but you own your workflow. Start by doing the following:

   - Document prompts that save time.
   - Automate repetitive data cleaning or reporting.
   - Teach one colleague how you built something with AI.
   - Give feedback on how tools or scripts could improve.
   - Create a small prompt library for your function.

   Impact starts at the edges. You don't need permission to improve the way you work.

2. **If you're a manager:** You have the power to set tone and direction. Start by doing the following:

   - Normalize the use of AI across the team.
   - Hold regular automation show-and-tell sessions.
   - Encourage experimentation and document what works.
   - Assign ownership of AI-based workflows.
   - Embed AI into goal-setting, reviews, or KPIs.

   You don't need to be the expert. You need to build the environment where experts can emerge.

3. **If you're a director or CFO:** You're positioned to remove friction and scale what works. Start by doing the following:

   - Identify where your team is spending time manually.
   - Remove approval friction for testing new tools.
   - Align with IT and legal on safe, compliant use.
   - Encourage cross-functional collaboration with data and ops.
   - Build a road map where AI is not a separate project, but a core capability.

   You don't need to chase tools. You need to build a system of enablement.

Bringing Stakeholders Along

Change doesn't happen in isolation. And AI can feel intimidating—especially for nontechnical or risk-sensitive stakeholders.

To lead effectively, you need to speak the language of your audience:

- **For IT:** Talk about governance, security, and auditability.
- **For finance leadership:** Talk about time savings, quality, and decision speed.
- **For risk and compliance:** Talk about constraints, reviews, and documentation.
- **For peers:** Talk about what works and how to try it safely.

AI transformation is not about heroics—it's about building trust. Use prompts like this:

"Write a short summary explaining our AI-based forecast automation. Include what it does, how it works, and how we review it."

Or:

"Write an FAQ document for internal finance teams explaining how we use AI responsibly."

Make the invisible logic visible.

Create Space for Experimentation

In fast-changing environments, experimentation beats planning. Here's what that looks like in practice:

- Give your team one to two hours per week for testing or learning.
- Use 10–20% of project time for automation or workflow redesign.

- Encourage "prototype first, perfect later" approaches.
- Share even half-finished improvements in a team channel.

And most important:

- **Celebrate small wins:** If someone automates a monthly task and saves 30 minutes—highlight it. If someone writes a cleaner prompt—ask them to share it. Build momentum by recognizing the behavior you want to spread.

This is how you shift from compliance-driven finance to capability-driven finance.

Evaluating AI Tools Responsibly

One of the most valuable roles you can play is filtering signal from noise.

AI tools will continue to emerge, and your team will ask, "Should we use this?"

Use the framework from earlier in this chapter:

- Can it reason well with financial logic?
- Does it handle numbers and structured data?
- Is it cost-effective, fast, and secure?
- Does it fit with our workflows and tools?
- Is it explainable? Can we audit it?

You don't need to say yes to everything. But when you say yes, you should know why.

And when you say no, explain it in terms of principles, not preferences.

You're not reading this book because you're afraid of change. You're reading it because you want to do better work, in smarter ways, with more impact.

That's what AI makes possible—not someday, but right now. You now know how to do the following:

- Use prompting to steer AI.
- Build forecasts, dashboards, models, and summaries with code generated for you.
- Automate workflows with Python, Power Query, and no-code platforms.
- Scale automation across your team.
- Evaluate new tools and lead responsibly.

But the biggest shift is this:

You're no longer just a finance professional who uses AI.
You're someone who knows how to build with it.

You're designing the next generation of finance. You're shaping what work looks like—for your team, your company, and yourself.

Let's keep building.

Chapter 10

Becoming an AI-Enabled Finance Leader

From Operator to Strategist—What AI Frees You to Focus On

One of the most common concerns finance professionals express about artificial intelligence (AI) is this:

"If AI can do the analysis, write the code, and generate the summary—what's left for me to do?"

It's a fair question. And an important one.
But it's also the wrong question.
The better question is:

"If AI can take care of the manual, technical, and repetitive parts of my work—what does that free me up to focus on?"

Because the truth is: AI doesn't replace finance professionals. It elevates them.

It moves you from operator to strategist.

In this section, we'll explore the following:

- How AI shifts the nature of finance work, not its value
- What AI can't replace—and why that's where your leadership matters most
- The strategic capabilities you can focus on once the execution is automated
- The opportunity to redesign your role and your team's function

AI Is Not the End of Finance Work—It's the End of the Mundane

Let's start by being clear about what AI is good at—and what it isn't. AI is excellent at these jobs:

- Writing code to clean or model data
- Generating summaries based on structured input
- Creating baseline reports and visuals
- Repeating tasks consistently and instantly
- Identifying patterns in historical data
- Responding quickly to prompts

But AI is not yet capable of the following:

- Understanding your business context the way you do
- Balancing conflicting priorities or stakeholder needs
- Framing trade-offs in complex decision environments
- Leading a conversation, influencing a room, or earning trust

These are the things only humans can do. And they're exactly the things that make finance leadership so valuable.

So the better way to think about this shift is this: *AI handles the baseline, so you can move upstream.*

You become less of a report generator—and more of a thought partner. Less focused on assembling data—and more focused on creating clarity.

From Execution to Insight

Traditionally, finance work has often been structured on execution:

- Close the books.
- Reconcile the accounts.
- Build the report.
- Refresh the forecast.
- Calculate the variance.
- Summarize the results.

Each of these steps has required time, precision, and focus.

But now, AI can handle many of them. The data refreshes itself. The summary is drafted. The variance is flagged automatically.

So the question becomes this:

"If the work is still being done—but not by you—what role do you play?"

Answer: *You play the role of interpreter, challenger, and advisor.*

You ask:

- What does this mean?
- How do we explain it?
- What actions should follow?
- What questions aren't being asked?
- What new scenario should we simulate?
- Where are we seeing early signals of change?

In other words: You stop delivering numbers, and start framing decisions.

Where You Add the Most Value

Let's break it down. Here are five areas where AI creates space for you to step up:

1. **Strategic framing:** Your ability to see the bigger picture becomes more important than ever. AI may show you the data—but only you can connect it to these areas:

    - Market dynamics
    - Organizational priorities
    - Customer behavior
    - Strategic initiatives

    Finance leaders must now help the business interpret complexity, not just measure it.

2. **Cross-functional influence:** AI doesn't sit in meetings. It doesn't negotiate budgets, clarify trade-offs, or advocate for resource allocation. You do.

    As a finance professional, your value lies in how well you can do the following:

    - Facilitate planning with Sales or Marketing.
    - Align initiatives with return on investment goals.
    - Help leadership think clearly under pressure.

    AI can support you—but it can't lead a cross-functional conversation.

3. **Scenario design:** AI can simulate—but only after you define the parameters.

    You still need to think about these issues:

    - What if revenue drops 20%?
    - What if we expand into this market?
    - What if our product mix shifts?

    Your job is to define what to model, why it matters, and how to interpret the outputs.

4. **Risk and judgment:** AI can quantify—but it can't assess reputational risk, political trade-offs, or cultural implications.

   You bring the human judgment that considers these issues:

   - What's technically optimal but politically sensitive
   - What's financially sound but operationally risky
   - What works on paper but not in practice

   This is why leadership is still human. Decisions happen in context, and AI doesn't have context.

5. **Narrative building:** AI can summarize—but it can't always tell the right story.

   Your communication becomes the multiplier:

   - Framing numbers in a way that drives action
   - Translating analytics into insights
   - Presenting options with clarity, not confusion

   You don't just answer questions—you shape how the business sees itself.

Redesigning Your Role

Once you embrace this mindset shift, you start seeing your work differently.

It's no longer about what you did—but what decisions you enabled.

It's not about how many hours you spent on a forecast—but what that forecast made possible.

In an AI-powered world, your role expand:

- Translator of complexity
- Designer of workflows
- Builder of capabilities
- Facilitator of insight
- Challenger of assumptions
- Partner to the business

The more you automate, the more strategic your role becomes—*if you step into it.*

When AI takes work off your plate, it's not a threat to your role—it's an invitation to upgrade it.

This is your moment to do the following:

- Focus on judgment, not just analysis.
- Invest in relationships, not just reconciliations.
- Spend time shaping the future, not just reporting the past.

You're not being replaced—you're being repositioned.

From operator to strategist. From builder of spreadsheets to builder of systems. From executor of tasks to enabler of outcomes.

Communicating Financial Intelligence with AI Support

One of the most overlooked shifts AI brings to finance work isn't in how we calculate—but in how we communicate.

Because for all the power in financial models, forecasts, dashboards, and reconciliations, none of it matters unless someone understands it. Unless someone takes action because of it.

This is where communication becomes the multiplier.

Finance teams are already being asked to do more than present data—they're being asked to explain it, frame it, and translate it into business terms.

Now, with the support of AI, you can take that to the next level.

Financial Communication Is a Leadership Skill

In an AI-enabled finance team, the real differentiator isn't who can build the model faster—it's who can make sense of it and communicate it clearly.

That's not about dumbing things down. It's about translating technical insight into practical direction.

Great communication in finance has the following qualities:

- Clear, not just correct
- Structured, not just verbose
- Audience-specific, not generic
- Narrative-driven, not just metric-heavy

This is where AI can help—but not replace—you.

AI can generate drafts, summaries, talking points, or slide content. But you still own the judgment and clarity.

How AI Can Support Communication in Finance

Here are the most common areas where AI can amplify your ability to communicate as a finance leader:

1. **Executive summaries:** You can use AI to do the following:

   - Review financial commentary and shorten it.
   - Highlight only key drivers.
   - Compare this month's story to last month's.
   - Suggest a tone that aligns with your stakeholder.

   Prompt example:

   "Summarize this P&L variance commentary for a CEO audience. Focus on high-level drivers and strip out technical details."

2. **Board reporting:** Board materials often require the following:

   - A crisp narrative
   - Strategic framing
   - Visual cues aligned to insight

   Prompt example:

   "Draft a slide summary for Q3 results. Include revenue, margin, and cost commentary. Keep it under 120 words, written in business language, not accounting terms."

3. **Emails and internal memos:** Instead of rewriting each update from scratch, ask AI to do the following:

- Format numbers into paragraphs.
- Adjust tone for different teams.
- Translate financial terms into plain English.

Prompt example:

"Write an internal email to the Sales team explaining why their forecast was reduced. Be clear but supportive, include numbers and a request for revalidation."

4. **Presentation scripts:** You can use AI to do the following:

- Draft talking points for forecast walkthroughs.
- Prepare Q&A scenarios.
- Frame transitions between data and recommendation.

Prompt example:

"Create a script to walk through this chart showing revenue vs budget over the last six months. Highlight key inflection points and what changed."

Adapting the Message to the Audience

One of the most important leadership skills is knowing how to change your message depending on who you're speaking to.

Finance data doesn't change. But its implications—and how you communicate them—do.

Let's look at a few audiences.

C-Suite (CEO, COO, CFO)

They want:

- Impact

- Trends
- Strategic options

Use AI to do the following:

- Summarize changes in a single paragraph.
- Suggest next steps or actions.
- Strip away technical explanations.

Operations and Department Heads

They want:

- Drivers
- Levers they can influence
- Clarification, not criticism

Use AI to do the following:

- Translate profit and loss (P&L) language into operational terms.
- Suggest questions they might ask.
- Create visuals or lists they can react to.

Investors and External Stakeholders

They want:

- Clarity
- Confidence
- Forward-looking insight

Use AI to do the following:

- Frame your numbers in narrative terms.
- Create comparable statements over time.
- Flag inconsistencies or gaps.

  Prompt example:

  "Rewrite this performance summary for an investor letter. Focus on growth, efficiency, and clarity. Use investor-appropriate language and remove internal terms."

Structuring the Story: Data → Insight → Action

AI is good at writing, but it still needs your logic.

Before you prompt for help communicating financial insights, think in terms of structure:

1. **Data**
   - What changed? What does the data show?
2. **Insight**
   - Why did it change? What does it mean?
3. **Action**
   - What should we do about it? What options exist?

This simple D-I-A structure helps you prompt with purpose. Example:

> "Use this revenue data and commentary. Write a D-I-A summary:

- Data: what happened
- Insight: why it happened
- Action: what decisions are needed next"

You can even ask:

> "Create two versions: one for executives, one for line managers."

Now you've built tailored financial communication at scale.

Repeatable Prompting for Financial Communication

To scale this capability across your team, treat your best communication prompts like templates.

Create a small library that includes prompts for the following:

- Monthly P&L summaries
- Forecast change explanations

- Budget presentations
- Variance root-cause walkthroughs
- Headcount or operating expenses updates
- Scenario recommendation framing

Encourage your team to do the following:

- Save what works.
- Improve what doesn't.
- Share successful examples.

Communication is not just a personal skill—it's a team capability.

These are some best practices for AI-assisted finance communication:

1. **Always edit AI outputs:** You are responsible for the message. Use AI for structure and drafts, not final word.
2. **Include context up front:** Tell the AI who the message is for, what tone to use, and what the goal is.
3. **Ask for multiple options:** Prompt for two to three variations. Choose the one that fits best.
4. **Use it to stress test your message:** Ask the AI, "What's missing?" or "What questions might this raise?"
5. **Keep a voice of leadership:** Let AI help you speak clearly—but make sure your voice leads.

AI won't speak for you—but it can help you speak more clearly, more quickly, and more consistently.

In a finance world where decision-making is accelerating, communication becomes more valuable—not less.

You're no longer just delivering reports. You're shaping how people interpret the business.

With AI as your support:

- You spend less time formatting and more time framing.
- You remove friction from executive communication.
- You help the organization move faster, with confidence.

Leading Change—Bringing People with You

Technology doesn't transform teams. People do.

No matter how powerful the tool or promising the technique, lasting change in a finance team only happens when people are brought along—intentionally, clearly, and humanely.

You've now seen what AI can do for forecasting, analysis, reporting, and decision support. But if your team isn't on board, the transformation won't stick.

AI Can Feel Like a Threat—Until It Feels Like a Tool

For many finance professionals, the rise of AI brings not just curiosity—but also discomfort.

You may have heard the following:

- "Will this replace my role?"
- "What if I fall behind?"
- "I'm not technical—how do I keep up?"
- "I've been doing it this way for years, why change now?"

These are valid concerns. And they're not solved by throwing a new tool into someone's inbox.

They're solved through leadership—through helping your team shift their mindset, upgrade their skill set, and see AI for what it really is: a tool that expands their capabilities, not a threat that erases their value.

Managing Resistance: What to Watch For

AI resistance often comes in subtle forms:

- **Quiet disengagement:** "I'll let others try this first."
- **Deflection:** "This isn't relevant to my role."
- **Overwhelm:** "There's too much changing at once."
- **Perfectionism:** "If I don't fully understand it, I won't use it."

You can't manage what you don't name. So the first step is to surface these mindsets in a respectful, low-stakes way.

Ask:

- "What are you curious about with AI right now?"
- "Where does it feel confusing or intimidating?"
- "What part of your workflow feels most repetitive?"
- "What have you seen that you wish you had time to try?"

When you invite people to share, without judgment, they're more likely to engage. When you model that learning is okay, others will follow.

Lead with Transparency, Not Hype

One of the biggest leadership mistakes in AI transformation is overselling.

Avoid saying:

- "This tool will change everything overnight."
- "You won't need to do these tasks anymore."
- "Just prompt the AI—it's simple."

Instead, tell the truth:

- "AI will take time to integrate, and that's okay."
- "You don't need to know everything. You just need to try something."
- "This is a capability we'll build together—not a box we check."

Leaders who are honest about the process—messy, nonlinear, imperfect—create psychological safety for their teams to experiment.

Coach Your Team to Grow with AI

Your job isn't to push tools. It's to coach capability.
That means:

- Helping team members identify where they spend too much time manually
- Encouraging them to build their first prompt, script, or automation—even if it's small
- Giving feedback not just on outputs, but on how they're learning
- Creating space for people to ask "dumb" questions without judgment

Ask:

- "What's one thing you'd like to automate next quarter?"
- "Want to try building that prompt together?"
- "Can we turn that into a repeatable script?"
- "What surprised you about what the AI got wrong?"

Make AI a team conversation—not a solo task.

Make AI Learning Part of the Workflow

One of the biggest barriers to adoption is time. If learning AI feels like extra work, it gets deprioritized.

Your job is to make it part of how work gets done—not something that only happens in training sessions.

Examples:

- In weekly meetings, have one team member share an AI win or experiment.
- Create a shared prompt library inside your financial planning and analysis (FP&A) or reporting folder.
- Treat process improvements like deliverables: "Automate one thing this quarter."
- Celebrate use—even if the prompt didn't work perfectly.

Small habits beat large initiatives.

AI adoption doesn't require a transformation team. It requires intentional rituals that signal *this matters now*.

Build a Culture of Curiosity, Not Compliance

There are two ways to approach change: enforce it or invite it.

Compliance might get short-term results, but curiosity creates momentum.

Encourage a curious mindset:

- "What else could we do with this?"
- "What if we tried prompting this analysis differently?"
- "How would an AI agent approach this workflow?"

Create room for experimentation:

- Give people time to test.
- Let them fail without penalty.
- Share early wins—even if they're messy.

And don't expect everyone to move at the same speed.

Some will adopt quickly. Others will hang back. That's okay.

As a leader, your job is to nurture progress, not enforce perfection.

Model the Mindset You Want to Spread

Teams follow what you do more than what you say.
If you do the following:

- Use AI in your own work.
- Share your prompts and improvements.
- Admit when the output wasn't perfect.
- Talk about what you're learning, not just what you know.

Then your team will feel permission to do the same.

Leadership is a mirror. If you're open, curious, and grounded—your team will be, too.

Change leadership in the AI era isn't about having all the answers. It's about creating the space for your team to find them.

You don't need to push people—you need to guide them.

You don't need to enforce tools—you need to normalize exploration.

You don't need to predict the future—you need to help your team build the skills to navigate it.

The teams that thrive in the years ahead won't be the ones with the fanciest models. They'll be the ones who do the following:

- Learn together.
- Share what works.
- Stay curious.
- Move forward—even when the tools keep changing.

Your Next 90 Days—Putting It All into Practice

Reading a book doesn't change your work.
Applying what you've read does.
You've now learned how to do the following:

- Use prompting to generate analysis, models, commentary, and automation.

- Apply Python, Power Query, and low-code tools across your FP&A workflows.
- Build automation into your processes, not just your tools.
- Lead others through AI-driven change.
- Communicate with clarity and influence using AI as your support.
- Think and operate like an AI-native finance professional.

But insight isn't enough. What you do in the next 90 days will determine whether this stays theoretical—or becomes transformational.

This final section is your practical implementation plan.

No jargon. No perfection required. Just focused, real-world momentum.

Why 90 Days?

Ninety days is long enough to make real changes—and short enough to keep urgency.

In 90 days, you can do the following:

- Reshape a workflow.
- Launch a small automation.
- Create a team prompt library.
- Test a new tool.
- Shift how your team approaches problem-solving.

It's not about doing everything at once. It's about starting in motion and creating early wins that scale.

Week 1–2: Assess and Align

1. **Pick a strategic use case:** Don't start with what's trendy—start with what's painful.

    Ask yourself or your team:
    - Where are we spending time manually?
    - What process breaks when it scales?
    - What task feels boring, repetitive, or high risk?

Pick one workflow that matters: reporting, forecasting, reconciliation, commentary. Make that your starting point.

2. **Assess AI readiness:** Look at your tools:

- Do you have access to a strong large language model (LLM) (e.g., ChatGPT, Gemini, Copilot)?
- Do you use Excel, Power BI, Python, or Power Query regularly?
- Is your data structured and consistent?

If not, can you sandbox something (e.g., clean dummy data, internal test) to experiment safely?

3. **Define the goal:** Be specific:

- "Reduce manual forecast update time by 50%."
- "Automate monthly variance commentary."
- "Create three reusable prompts for QBR deck creation."
- "Keep it narrow. Focus beats ambition at this stage."

Week 3–5: Build, Prompt, and Automate

4. **Write the first prompts:** Start small and specific. Use the prompting frameworks from Chapters 2 and 3.

Examples:

- "Summarize this Excel table into monthly P&L commentary."
- "Generate Python code that merges two datasets and flags outliers."
- "Write a Slack message explaining a forecast update to our VP of Sales."

Save, revise, and document what works.

5. **Create a repeatable workflow:** Once you have a working prompt or script, make it part of your process:

- Add it to your month-end checklist.
- Use it in your next planning cycle.
- Share it in your team's reporting folder.

This is how experiments become systems.

6. **Build in light automation:** If the task is recurring, automate it:

- Python script that runs weekly
- Power Query that refreshes with one click
- Zapier or n8n flow that sends alerts or updates dashboards

Use AI to help you write the automation logic—and test with sample data first.

Week 6–8: Share, Train, Expand

7. **Build a prompt library:** Every time a prompt works, save it.

Create a folder or doc with the following:

- Prompt text
- Example input/output
- Tool used (e.g., Python, Excel, ChatGPT)
- Notes or variations

Encourage others to contribute. This becomes your team's AI playbook.

8. **Run a team session:** Host a short meeting or async discussion:

- Share your results.
- Walk through a prompt or script.
- Ask teammates where they'd like to try using AI.
- Offer to help with setup or testing.

The goal isn't to train everyone overnight. It's to normalize progress and create momentum.

9. **Document and reflect:** AI transformation isn't just about velocity—it's about clarity.

Ask:

- What did we try?
- What worked?
- What failed—and why?
- What should we improve next cycle?

Use AI to help you summarize your own progress:

> "Write a short internal report summarizing our AI experimentation over the last six weeks."

Week 9–12: Operationalize and Scale

10. **Embed into core workflows:** Choose at least one process where AI becomes the standard, not the experiment.

Examples:

- Forecasts are updated using a prompt template.
- Variance commentary is auto-drafted monthly.
- A specific Slack report is triggered automatically after close.
- Scenario analysis is run with AI-assisted Python scripts.

Don't wait for perfection. Go live, review, and iterate.

11. **Set KPIs for AI use:** Start measuring the impact of your work:

- Time saved per report
- Errors reduced in reconciliations
- Number of reusable prompts/scripts created
- Speed from data to decision

Create your own AI adoption dashboard. Share wins openly. Success is contagious.

12. Create your AI capability map: Now look ahead. Ask:

- What do we want every team member to be capable of?
- What tools should we invest in next?
- What guardrails or standards do we need?
- This is how you evolve from AI experiments to AI maturity.

Final Thoughts: Start Small, Think Long

You don't need to automate your entire function overnight.

You don't need to know everything about LLMs, Python, or M code.

You just need to do the following:

- Pick a real use case.
- Write a prompt that solves part of it.
- Test, improve, and share.
- Build a habit of experimentation.
- Lead others by showing what's possible.

Every transformation starts with one small, useful action.

In 90 days, you won't just know more about AI—you'll have built something that works.

And that's what leadership in the AI era looks like:

- Not waiting for change
- Not guessing what's coming
- But building the systems, habits, and teams to shape it

Let's go do the work.

About the Author

Christian Martinez is the Global Senior Finance Transformation senior manager at Kraft Heinz and an AI for Finance professor. With more than a decade of experience across multinational organizations, he has built his career in diverse international markets including the Netherlands, Australia, and Mexico. Throughout his professional journey, Christian has developed deep expertise in financial planning and analysis (FP&A), finance transformation, and finance analytics, leading large-scale initiatives that modernize finance functions and bring data-driven decision-making to the forefront.

His work spans strategic business partnering, cross-functional collaboration, and advising senior FP&A leaders and C-suite executives on the adoption of AI, automation, and data analytics.

As an industry thought leader, Christian is a distinguished international speaker who has delivered sessions at renowned events such as the World Finance Forum, World Summit AI, Finance Digitalization Forum, and the EMEA FP&A Summit.

His passion for education has driven him to train more than 20,000 senior finance professionals through courses, workshops, and corporate programs, helping leaders worldwide navigate the evolving landscape of AI in finance.

Christian's work has earned him significant recognition, including being named among the "30 Under 30" in accounting and finance in Australia (2021), the EMEA Data Democratizer Award (2022), the International Rising Star in Finance Award (2023), and most recently, Finance Leader of the Year by GenCFO (2024).

Beyond his professional life, Christian is an avid marathon finisher and an enthusiastic world traveler—having explored more than 70 countries—which fuels his curiosity, discipline, and global perspective.

Index

A
adaptability, to AI, 19
Advanced AI for Finance program, 4
agents, AI, 6, 205, 208, 212–213, 245
   definition, 213–214
   risks and limitations, 216–218
   technology, 215–216
   use cases, 214–215
AI. *See* artificial intelligence (AI)
AI-enabled decision frameworks, 174
AI-enabled finance leader
   audience message, 238–239
   coach capability, 244
   communicating financial
      intelligence with, 236
   curious mindset, 245
   finance work, 232
      structured on execution, 233
   financial communication, 236–238
      D-I-A structure, 240
      repeatable prompting, 240–242
   lasting change in finance team, 242
   leadership mistakes in transformation, 243–244
   mindset model, 246
   from operator to strategist, 231–232
   practical implementation planning, 246–251
   resistance management, 243
   steps
      cross-functional influence, 234
      narrative building, 235
      reputational risk, 235
      scenario design, 234
      strategic framing, 234
   threat, 242
   workflow learning, 244–245
AI-generated Python, 121, 122, 161
   correlation, clustering, and attribution analysis, 112–117
   prompting technique, 60–64
AI-native finance team, 205, 218–221
AI-powered world, 235–236
analytics, powered by AI
   descriptive, 15
   diagnostic, 15–16
   predictive, 16–17
   prescriptive, 17–18

INDEX

API authentication, 4
ARIMA. *See* AutoRegressive Integrated Moving Average (ARIMA)
artificial intelligence (AI), 7
  descriptive analytics
    audiences, 98–99
    balancing automation and judgment, 101
    channels, 100–101
    dashboard, 99–100
    from data to message, 97
    outputs, 96–97
    prompting for storytelling, 98
    slide-ready content, 99
  diagnostic analytics, 103–105, 124
    correlation, clustering, and attribution, 112–117
    hypothesis generation, 110
    mindset, 107–108
    prompting and interpreting, 118
    Python, 105–107
    questions with, 108–109
    repeatable system, 118–123
    structuring, 109
    text prompting, 110–112
    without losing ownership, 123–124
  in finance, 1–3
  finance stack
    agents, 212–214 (*see also* agents)
    AI-native finance team, 218–221
    approach, 211–212
    cross-functional partnerships, 222
    fast-changing experimentation, 227–228
    feedback loops in workflows, 222–223
    future proof, 224–225
    high-functioning AI-native teams, 223–224
    hiring, 221
    landscape changes, 207–208
    LLMs, 209–210
    nontechnical finance professional, 215–216
    nontechnical/risk-sensitive stakeholders, 227
    onboarding curriculum, 221–222
    problem-solvers interview, 221
    side-by-side comparison, 209
    tools, 211, 228–229
    from tool user to system designer, 225
    transformation, 224, 226
    use cases, 214–215
  predictive analytics (*see* predictive analytics, AI)
  prescriptive analytics, 151–154
    AI-enabled decision frameworks, 174
    auditable and transparent decision support, 173–174
    building blocks, 153
    decision frameworks, 169–170
    decision-making assistant, 156–157
    decision matrix, 170–171
    draft executive recommendations, 171–172
    finance professionals, 152
    from forecasting to decision-making, 151
    from forecast outputs to action inputs, 155–156
    if-then statements, 155
    Monte Carlo simulation, 163–166, 168
    optimization modeling using Python, 157–159
    optimization outputs, 162
    prompting style, 154–155
    PuLP, 159–160
    scipy.optimize, 160–161
    simulation modeling, 163, 167–169
    trade-off narratives, 171
    visualization and communication, 162
attribution techniques, 112, 113, 115–117
auditable decision support, 173–174
automated report distribution, 197
automating descriptive reporting
  Excel, 92–94
  Power BI, 94–95
  with Python, 91–92
automation workflows, Python, 70–71
autonomous finance tooling, 212–213
AutoRegressive Integrated Moving Average (ARIMA), 135–138

Index

B
base case, 140, 141
best case, 140, 141
board reporting, 237
Boucher, Nicolas, 4
browser-based Python, 186–187
budget allocation, 160–162
building scenario models, 3, 12

C
cash flow simulation, 165–166
CEO, 46, 47, 49, 53, 237, 238
CFO. *See* chief financial officer (CFO)
ChatGPT, 4, 6, 9–11, 13, 15, 17, 18, 21, 44,
    58, 59, 76, 80, 83, 104, 189, 201, 207,
    211, 218, 248–249
ChatGPT 3.5, 4, 18
chief financial officer (CFO), 2, 4, 5, 11, 22,
    28, 31–32, 42, 43, 53, 59, 71, 87, 96,
    98, 100, 123, 126, 149, 167, 172, 173,
    197, 213, 224, 226, 238
Claude, 9, 22, 58, 208
Claude 2, 18
clustering technique, 112–115
coach capabilities, 244
code generation, 12, 110–112
comma-separated values (CSV), 128, 133,
    143, 180, 181, 183, 184, 187, 191
continuous learning, 144–145
Copilot, 6, 9, 10, 15, 18, 21, 44, 58, 75, 80,
    92–95, 183, 189, 201, 202, 208, 210,
    211, 218, 248
correlation techniques, 112–114
cross-functional influence, 234
cross-functional partnerships, 222
C-Suite, 238–239, 253
CSV. *See* comma-separated values (CSV)

D
dashboard refresh notification, 197
dash, Python scripts, 70
data processing agent, 215
data transformation, 12, 90, 190
decision-making assistant, 156–157
decision matrix, 170–171
descriptive analytics, 15, 71, 79–80
AI in, 83–84
    commentary, 84–85
    performance summaries, 84–85
    prompting for commentary, 86
audiences, 98–99
balancing automation and judgment, 101
channels, 100–101
dashboard, 99–100
from data to message, 97
definition, 80–81
outputs, 96–97
prompting for storytelling, 98
slide-ready content, 99
strategic finance, 82
tools in finance, 81
descriptive prompt, 154–155
diagnostic analytics, 15–16, 81, 102–104,
    107, 111, 118, 124
D-I-A structure, 240
distributed automation, 202–203
driver-based model, 139, 141

E
emails, 238
enterprise resource planning (ERP)
    systems, 73, 81, 91, 196, 208, 214
ERP systems. *See* enterprise resource
    planning (ERP) systems
Excel, 2, 3, 11–15, 18, 19, 50–52, 55, 58–64,
    66, 67, 69, 71–77, 83, 90–96, 100,
    126, 132, 143–144, 149, 153, 160,
    179–190, 194, 196, 198–199, 201,
    205, 208, 210, 248, 249
no-code flows, 198–199
with Python, 73–74
step-by-step automation flow, 192–193
expense approval flow, 198
external stakeholders, 239

F
Facebook (Meta), 68, 133
fast-changing experimentation,
    227–228
feedback loops
    forecast accuracy, 147–148
    workflows, 222–223

INDEX

few-shot learning, 26–27
finance function, 5, 6, 178, 201–202, 253
finance logic model, 130–131
finance professionals, 1–5, 12, 13, 18, 19, 181
  analysis prompts, 40–41
  conversation, 48
  effective prompt engineering techniques
    ambiguity, 35–36
    constraints and guardrails, 36–37
    context information, 28–29
    few-shot learning, 26–27
    iterative questioning, 34–35
    output formatting prompts, 32–33
    reasoning step-by-step, 27–28
    ROI, 30–31
    role prompting, 31–32
    split complex questions, 29–30
  failed prompts, 46
  FP&A, 37
  hallucinations, 45–46
  high-performing prompts, 49–50
  inputs and outputs in tokens, 23–24
  instruction vs completion-based prompts, 25
  iteration, 44, 47–48
  large language models (LLMs), 21–23
  organizing prompts, 51–52
  parallel prompting strategy, 49
  planning prompts, 37–38
  practices, 53–54
  professional skill, 54–55
  from prompt to PowerPoint, 43–44
  reasoning models, 24
  reporting prompts, 39–40
  templates, 52–53
  writing commentary, 41–43
finance stack, AI
  agents, 212–214 (*see also* agents)
  AI-native finance team, 218–221
  approach, 211–212
  cross-functional partnerships, 222
  fast-changing experimentation, 227–228
  feedback loops in workflows, 222–223
  future proof, 224–225
  high-functioning AI-native teams, 223–224
  hiring, 221
  landscape changes, 207–208
  LLMs, 209–210
  nontechnical finance professional, 215–216
  nontechnical/risk-sensitive stakeholders, 227
  onboarding curriculum, 221–222
  problem-solvers interview, 221
  side-by-side comparison, 209
  tools, 211, 228–229
  from tool user to system designer, 225
  transformation, 224, 226
  use cases, 214–215
finance work, structured on execution, 233
financial communication, 236–238
  D-I-A structure, 240
  leadership skill, 236–237
  repeatable prompting, 240–242
financial planning and analysis (FP&A), 1, 37, 151, 245
  applying prompting to workflow, 37
  automation, 177–178, 205
    browser-based Python, 186–187
    culture, 199–200
    distributed automation, 202–203
    finance function, 201–202
    finance professionals, 181
    finance work, 196
    financial workflows, 179
    framework, 181–182
    good automation candidate, 180
    low-code automation, 194–195
    manual processing, 178
    mindset, 182–183, 200
    Power BI, 193
    Power Query (*see* Power Query)
    prompt library, 200–201
    Python, 181, 183–185 (*see also* Python)
    risk, 203
    template, 202
    workflows, 204
  scenario forecasting, 140–141
financial workflows, 175, 179

Index

forecasting. *See* predictive analytics, AI
FP&A. *See* financial planning and analysis (FP&A)

G

Gemini, 6, 9, 22, 44, 58, 80, 104, 208, 211, 248
Gemini 2.5, 10, 18
Generative AI, 2, 6, 9–10
good automation candidate, 180
Google Colab, 13, 17, 59, 61–64, 72–73, 76, 106, 115, 133, 140, 149, 182–184, 186, 188, 196, 198
GPT-4, 22–24, 208
GPT-4o, 10, 18

H

hallucinations, 27, 30, 45–46, 89, 217
hard-coded models, 141–142
high-functioning AI-native teams, 223–224
high-performing prompts, 49–50
high-value diagnostic patterns, 119–120
human judgment, 121, 125, 235
hypothesis generation, 108, 110

I

if-then statements, 155
information technology (IT), 2, 70–72, 74, 110, 177, 195, 221, 222, 226, 227
instruction vs completion-based prompts, 25
internal memos, 238
investors stakeholders, 239
IT. *See* information technology (IT)

K

key performance indicators (KPIs), 81, 204, 216, 226, 250

L

large language models (LLMs), 10–11, 13, 15, 17, 18, 21–24, 27, 28, 31, 80, 85, 89, 125, 179, 208–210, 248, 251
leadership mistakes, in transformation, 243–244
leadership skill, 236–238
light automation, 249

linear programming library, 159–160
line chart, forecasting, 142–143
LLaMA, 10, 208
LLMs. *See* large language models (LLMs)
low-code automation, 194–197
  workflows, 196–198

M

machine learning (ML), 4, 58, 66, 68–69, 79
  reinforcement learning, 9
  supervised learning, 8
  types of, 8–9
  unsupervised learning, 8–9
MAE. *See* Mean Absolute Error (MAE)
Make (formerly Integromat), 194–196
MAPE. *See* Mean Absolute Percentage Error (MAPE)
matplotlib, 60, 64, 69, 73, 115, 129, 130, 140, 165
Mean Absolute Error (MAE), 145, 146
Mean Absolute Percentage Error (MAPE), 144–149
Microsoft Copilot, 6, 9, 10, 15, 18, 21, 44, 58, 75, 80, 92–95, 183, 189, 201, 202, 208, 210–211, 218, 248
mindset model, 246
ML. *See* machine learning (ML)
Monte Carlo simulation, 163–166, 168

N

narrative building, 235
n8n, 6, 52, 149, 175, 183, 194–198, 200, 201, 214, 215, 249
no-code movement, 194–195
nontechnical finance professionals, 215–216
nontechnical stakeholders, 227
numpy, 67, 128, 129, 165

O

o3, 10
onboarding curriculum, 221–222
OpenAI, 4, 24, 215
OpEx, 108, 110, 113, 119, 122, 152–155
optimization modeling, Python, 157–159
optimization outputs, 162, 174

P

pandas, 61, 62, 66, 67, 92, 111, 114, 128, 129, 140, 146, 165, 185
parallel prompting strategy, 49
plotly, 69–70
political trade-offs, 235
Power BI, 12, 15, 90–92, 94–96, 99, 100, 183, 188–191, 193, 194, 196, 197, 201, 208, 210, 214, 248
    automation, 194
Power Query, 6, 52, 93, 95, 175, 177, 182, 183, 188–193, 200, 203, 205
    errors, 191–192
    Excel data, 192–193
    M code, 191
practical fluency, 19
practical implementation planning, 246–251
predictive analytics, AI, 16–17
    forecasting, 125–126, 150
        actuals and forecasts for revenue, 146–147
        AutoRegressive Integrated Moving Average (ARIMA), 135–138
        communication, 149
        dashboard evaluation, 147
        driver-based model, 141
        evaluation, 144–146, 148–149
        with feedback loops, 147–148
        finance logic and statistical models, 130–131
        FP&A, scenario forecasting, 140–141
        hard-coded models, 141–142
        line chart, 142–143
        model, 127–128
        Python, 128–130
        scenario modeling, 143–144
        seasonality and holidays, 134–135
        Streamlit app, 143
        time series forecasting with Python, 131–132
        traditional forecasting limitations, 126–127
        visualization, 136
prescriptive analytics, 17–18, 151–154
    AI-enabled decision frameworks, 174
    auditable and transparent decision support, 173–174
    building blocks, 153
    decision frameworks, 169–170
    decision-making assistant, 156–157
    decision matrix, 170–171
    draft executive recommendations, 171–172
    finance professionals, 152
    from forecasting to decision-making, 151
    from forecast outputs to action inputs, 155–156
    if-then statements, 155
    Monte Carlo simulation, 163–166, 168
    optimization modeling using Python, 157–159
    optimization outputs, 162
    prompting style, 154–155
    PuLP, 159–160
    scipy.optimize, 160–161
    simulation modeling, 163, 167–169
    trade-off narratives, 171
    visualization and communication, 162
prescriptive prompt, 155
presentation scripts, 238
pricing strategy simulation, 166
problem-solvers interview, 221
product mix optimization, 161
prompt engineering, 22
    for analysis, 40–41
    applying to FP&A workflows, 37
    core techniques, 26
        ask for explanations before answers, 30–31
        avoid ambiguity, 35–36
        chain-of-thought, 27–28
        few-shot learning, 26–27
        include context information, 28–29
        iterative questioning, 34–35
        output formatting prompts, 32–33
        role prompting, 31–32
        split complex tasks, 29–30
        use constraints and guardrails, 36–37
    definition, 22
    frameworks, 248

instruction following *versus* completion-based, 22–25
iterating prompts, 44
library, 50–51
models reasoning, 24
organizing by function, 51–52
parallel prompting strategy, 49
for planning, 37–38
PowerPoint, 43–44
prompt library, 50–51
refine a prompt based on errors, 45–46
repeatable prompting system, 50
for reporting, 39–40
reusing high-performing prompts, 49–50
using prompt templates, 52–53
to write commentary, 41–43
to write emails, 41–43
to write executive summaries, 41–43
Prophet, 17, 68, 73, 77, 130, 132–137
PuLP, 158–161
Python, 4, 12–14, 177, 179, 181–186, 200, 205
automation workflows with, 71–76
diagnostic analytics, 105–107
in Excel, 73–74
in finance, 65–70
forecasting, 128–130
Google Colab, 72–73
no-code flows, 198–199
optimization modeling using, 157–159
Power Query, 189–191
scheduling with, 187–189
time series forecasting with, 131–132
Visual Studio Code (VS Code), 75–76
workflows with, 70–71

Q
quarter-end checklist automation, 198

R
reinforcement learning, 9
reputational risk, 235
resistance management, 243
risk-sensitive stakeholders, 227
RMSE. *See* Root Mean Squared Error (RMSE)
ROI, 133, 154, 158–160, 162, 171
effective prompt engineering techniques, 30–31
rolling forecast agent, 214
Root Mean Squared Error (RMSE), 144, 146

S
scenario design, 234
scikit-learn, 68–69, 73
scipy.optimize, 160–161
seaborn, 69, 73, 114, 115, 130
self-driving finance, 212–213
self-healing automation agent, 215
simulation modeling, 163, 167–169
smoothing-based forecast, 129
SMTP, 187
statistical models, 10, 118, 130–131
Streamlit app, 70, 143, 149
supervised learning, 8, 9

T
team session, 249
text generation, 4, 12
text prompting, 110–112
thresholds, slack alerts, 197
time series forecasting
components, 132
to driver-based models, 139–140
fbprophet, 133–134
with Python and AI, 131–132
scenario forecasting, 138–139
structuring, 137
tokens, 22–25, 210
transformers architecture, 11
transparent decision support, 173–174

U
unsupervised learning, 8–9

V
variance investigation agent, 214
Visual Studio Code (VS Code), 13, 59, 72, 75–76
VS Code. *See* Visual Studio Code (VS Code)

W

workflow automation, 12, 204
workflows feedback loops, 222–223
workflows learning, 244–245
workforce planning, 161
working prompt/script, 249
worst case, 140, 141

Y

yfinance library, 67

Z

Zapier, 149, 194–196, 215